"This book will enrich your outlook on golf and life. It's filled with great homespun golf humor and enough personal experiences to keep you smiling for a week. Most importantly, it will help all golfers develop a stronger personal relationship with Jesus on and off the course."

Wally Armstrong, PGA Tour player, teacher,
and author of *The Heart of a Golfer*

"This book is a kick in the pants! Phil Callaway transitions seamlessly from the golf course to everyday life. One minute he gets me carefully considering my faith, and the next minute he's got me laughing out loud! I highly recommend this book."

Casey Martin, pro golfer
and men's golf coach, University of Oregon

"Playing golf with Phil Callaway is almost as much fun as reading this book. I laughed. I almost cried. I even forgot about my score. And when I least expected it, I learned something. If you're anything like me, you'll want to keep several copies of this book in your golf bag for inspiration. Or to give out to people when you forget to yell 'Fore!'"

Ken Davis, bestselling author and speaker

"I've golfed with Phil, and he needs money for lessons. So buy armloads of this book. Give them out to friends and complete strangers. Amid the laughter they'll discover timeless principles that will change their game and their lives."

Mike Yorkey, coauthor of the Every Man series

"Making sense of my golf game is like trying to understand the purpose of pain. Golf can be enraging, humiliating, and exhilarating all at once. I make just enough good shots to keep me coming back for more. I hoped this book would help me make sense of my golf game, but it healed something far deeper. Plain and simple—'Philosopher Phil's' insights on the emotional and spiritual sides of life make sense. This is a must-read for anyone trying to grasp the meaning of life as seen through the game of golf."

Joel Freeman, motivational guru, author, and
former NBA chaplain of the Washington Bullets

"The majority of my life I've been a competitive person learning life lessons from the game of hockey. Phil Callaway has shown me how the game of golf (another favorite of mine) demonstrates patience, perseverance, and integrity—all characteristics God desires in our life. This book is an entertaining read that will have you laughing out loud (except for his comments on hockey in chapter 25!) while challenging you with the things that matter most."

Shane Doan, former captain, Phoenix Coyotes

"Even if you think playing golf is a bit less fun than mall-walking, you're about to gain a new appreciation of the sport. Funny things happen to Phil when he plays golf, and he has a great time telling of his adventures and misadventures—whether playing on a homemade course or an actual course with flagsticks and everything. But beyond the humor and the tongue-in-cheek insistence that golf is the greatest sport on earth (has Phil never played basketball?), Callaway intersperses his lightheartedness with a healthy helping of biblical truth and godly wisdom. Each story points the reader toward a life of Christlikeness and faith—something every duffer who ever drowned a golf ball needs to accomplish."

Dave Branon, Sports Spectrum, and
writer for *Our Daily Bread*

"Phil's golf stories will touch the heart of every golfer, but his spiritual message is the best of all."

Bearcat Murray, former trainer, Calgary Flames

"Phil Callaway finds ways to push life lessons through a tunnel of laughter. My funny bone gets tickled even while I'm focused on the game Mark Twain suggested was little more than 'a good walk ruined.'"

Ryan Walter, sports broadcaster, Stanley Cup champion

Under Par

PHIL CALLAWAY

HARVEST HOUSE PUBLISHERS
EUGENE, OREGON

Cover design by Bryce Williamson

Cover photo © Fourleaflover, nicoolay, aleksandarvelasevic, Tuleedin, Inna Sinano / Gettyimages

Interior design by Rockwell Davis

Under Par
Previously published as *Golfing with the Master*, with extensive revisions and new material
Copyright © 2020 by Phil Callaway
Published by Harvest House Publishers
Eugene, Oregon 97408
www.harvesthousepublishers.com

ISBN 978-0-7369-7922-1 (pbk.)
ISBN 978-0-7369-7923-8 (eBook)

Library of Congress Cataloging-in-Publication Data is on file at the Library of Congress, Washington, DC.

Printed in the United States of America

20 21 22 23 24 25 26 27 28 / BP-RD / 10 9 8 7 6 5 4 3 2 1

For ten grandchildren under five
who are too young to golf yet
but make me laugh when they try.
I love you even more than golf.

CONTENTS

THE INVITATION

Some moments you never forget. The birth of a child. The death of a dog. The yes from a woman who will love you for life. I have experienced all three. When my son Stephen was ten, we shared another unforgettable moment. For the first time ever he saw his dad stroll into the clubhouse under par.

My clubs were batons in the hands of a great maestro that day. The greens threw out welcome mats. The fairways yawned widely. Balls—once wayward—funneled toward the hole and leaped into the cup like reunited lovers. I could do no wrong.

They say that less than 3 percent of golfers ever finish under par. A handful of times I have joined them. On each occasion I found myself humbly telling a friend or 12 about it. "Yeah, so I...uh...finished under par." A few were stunned. All were impressed. One said, "I'm sorry to hear that." To him "under par" meant "worse than expected," "subpar," "not very good." As in, "That ham and egg sandwich was under par. I'm feeling a little under par since eating it."

I have experienced both meanings of the term *under par*. I imagine you have too. There are moments we celebrate and moments we tolerate. Days when life's fairways are wide as a yawn and days they're as narrow as a keyhole. Exhilaration and exasperation. Mountaintops and valleys. Maternity wards and cancer wards. Life and golf can be cruel and wonderful. In this book you'll find stories of friendship, hardship, failure, and grace. Whether or not you share my Christian faith, I think these stories will help you laugh and celebrate. They may tug at your tear ducts too.

Of course, it was necessary to conduct extensive research for this book. So I called my sons and my friends and hit the links—slicing, duffing, laughing, and telling stories. It was grueling work. By summer's end three things had happened.

First, I contracted a severe case of golfer's tan. When I walked from the changing room to the pool, teenagers wrinkled their pierced eyebrows at my leathery neck, my tanned legs, and what appeared to be little white socks.

Second, I shaved four strokes from my handicap with a few simple tips and tricks I'll be happy to share with you.

Third—and best of all—I came to better understand 36 life lessons this glorious and frustrating game can teach us if we listen. Principles that can help us get our lives back on course, focus on stuff that matters, and celebrate the golfer's favorite four-letter word—*hope*—even on cloudy days.

Thanks for joining me. Grab your clubs, maestro. Looks like we're up.

1

THE ITCH

Golf is so popular simply because it is the best
game in the world at which to be bad.

A.A. MILNE

I've had it with winter. It's the middle of April, and dirty brown snowdrifts are hanging on, smothering the grass and choking the life out of the tulips. The thermometer claims it's 36 degrees. That's generous. Like my childhood dentist poking his head into the waiting room, winter keeps coming back, looking for victims.

I have done all I can to ease the pain. I putt in the living room. And chip onto the sofa. I watch the Golf Channel and flip through a coffee-table book—*100 Courses You Can Play*—aware that I can't play a one of them.

On the windward side of the Hawaiian island of Oahu is the Ko'olau Golf Course. It mocks me from these colorful pages. Considered by many to be the toughest course on earth, Ko'olau is set within an ancient volcano. Locals have dubbed it "King Kong in a grass skirt." "Monster Mash." "Beauty and the Beast." They advise bringing twice as many balls as you have strokes in your handicap. The course record is 69. Lost balls, that is.

I don't care. I'd golf the Sahara right now. Bring it on. Sand traps aren't that bad. Christopher Columbus went around the world in 1492. That's not a bad score when you think about it.

I phone my friends Vance and Ron. "I can't take it anymore," I whine. "I'm pulling my clubs out of cold storage. Let's go."

The clubhouse is dark and silent when we arrive. Lenny, the greens keeper, is busily mending the bridge that links the creek to the practice green. I chat with him about the level of the water, the health of his family, the clubs he got for Christmas. But he's not dumb. He knows why I'm here. I'm like a bird dog pointing at the first tee. "I'm a lifer, Lenny," I finally plead. "Surely I can get on a wee bit early." He laughs and points at the fairway on two. "There's a lake on it," he says. "It's large enough to host a floatplane. If you go out there, we'll have to form a search party."

I glance over at Vance and Ron, who are waiting patiently in the van, their noses pressed against the frosty glass.

"How about a bucket of range balls?" I beg, hoping Lenny will throw me some scraps.

"Sure." He smiles, waving at my friends. "Just don't slip on the skating rink there on the left."

We cross the bridge eagerly, each of us lugging a well-rounded bucket. Long months of winter fade into memory as we trudge through the muck laughing like kids on Christmas morning. Tired golf jokes are funny once more. "Tell the Drag Harry joke," Ron says.

Ragged clouds scatter overhead allowing the sun to poke through. Silver linings are everywhere.

"See that sand trap by the 150-yard marker?" I point.

"That's no sand trap. That's a snowdrift."

"Come on. Use your imagination."

"Let's try to hit it," says Vance.

"Okay. You first, then it's my turn," says Ron.

"We'll shoot until someone lands in the trap," says Vance. "Loser hits the rest of his bucket with his shirt off."

"You're on," I say. I can beat these guys blindfolded.

The first day of the season my golf game surprises me. My swing hasn't had time to know any better. Sure, there's rust on it, but with enough low expectations, I am tremendous. Teeing one up, I chip it toward the snow trap, tingling with anticipation at the long summer stretching before me.

Watching the ball take flight, I remember why I love this game.

There's the majestic scenery, of course. But it goes far deeper.

I love the stillness out here. The talks with my sons as we search for my ball. I love the way this game teaches humility. Not always, but often. I love the smell of freshly mown grass and the reminder that life is a walk, not a sprint.

I love the way golf brings my sins bubbling to the surface like no other sport, reminding me of bad habits that need breaking, rough edges that need smoothing.

I love the camaraderie of a Texas Scramble, of best ball. Perhaps it's the closest some of us get to a church, a place where we care about the other guy's swing, where we cheer each other on.

I love the discipline of working at something I know I can improve upon. The hope I feel before each swing.

I love the amusing grace of a mulligan.

Of course, there's the embarrassment of forgetting I have golf shoes on and standing at the checkout line in our small town's one and only grocery store with little kids pointing at the "funny old man" who writes those books. But today even that makes me smile.

This year I'll make a concerted effort to complain less. To

appreciate what I have. It's one of the best clubs you can have in your bag.

They say God's faithfulness is like the seasons. That "as long as the earth remains, there will be planting and harvest, cold and heat, winter and summer, day and night."[1] It's the hope every October golfer clings to where I come from.

"Hey," says Vance. "What are you smiling about? It's your turn."

I'm smiling because the warm winds of May are coming. I'll beat these guys then. But for now, I'll finish this bucket and then put on my shirt.

Those who appreciate life find they have more of it.

Tip of the Day: Always warm up. If time is short, forget the range. Swing two clubs together and stretch. Chip and putt a bit. Drop a ball two feet from the cup, another a foot farther out, and then a few more. Start close, and then move out only when you sink one. Start over when you miss. This way you can save $3 a day on range balls. In the average lifetime that's more than $87,000.

2

WHAT DRIVES YOU?

I'm a golfaholic, no question about that. Counseling wouldn't help me. They'd have to put me in prison, and then I'd talk the warden into building a hole or two and teach him how to play.

LEE TREVINO

Some of us worship in churches, some in synagogues, some on golf courses.

ADLAI STEVENSON

For some golf is an obsession. They would play Mount Everest if someone put a flagstick on it. They arrive at the office wearing a Jordan Spieth shirt ("Full Spieth Ahead"), work an hour or two, hang up a sign that says, "Gone fishing for golf balls," and then vamoose. I even heard of a wife who got after her husband for teeing off before eight in the morning. He used a lob wedge from the living room carpet and shattered a lamp.

After writing the book *With God on the Golf Course*, I received an avalanche of email from relatives of golf nuts. Some were from good, law-abiding citizens who viewed golfers with all the warmth they normally reserve for tax auditors (except they believe tax auditors are useful people).

Here's one of those letters, slightly edited to protect the guilty:

> I've been married to a golf nutsoid for twenty-one years, and I've about had it. He plays golf five times a week, and when he comes home he watches it. Then he reads about it. We're having dinner with friends, and somehow it always comes up. In the past, my son kept me company when his dad was playing golf. Now he goes with him. Last week my husband showed up with a gift for me. I was so excited. Then I opened it. I can't believe they make a "What Would Rory Do?" bracelet. I think it's called golf because all the other four-letter words were taken. I think golf stands for "Go Out, Leave Family." When I die, bury me on the golf course. It's the only way my husband will visit me. What should I do? Don't dare tell me to start playing golf!
>
> Sincerely, Frosted in Florida.

If you're concerned that you may be following in this guy's footsteps, here are some warning signs on the road to becoming a golfaholic:

- You are playing golf and it is raining.
- You are unable to count past five.
- You are playing golf and it is snowing.
- Lightning only encourages you.
- You are playing golf and it is Christmas morning.
- Or your twenty-fifth anniversary.
- You live to shoot your age.

- Then you live to shoot your weight.

The Golf Nut Society is a social network celebrating obsessed golfers. It recently bestowed its coveted "Golf Nut of the Year" award to a guy who spent his honeymoon playing 36 holes a day. Spoiler alert: his marriage didn't last.

I much prefer the way Jordan Spieth lists his priorities: "My faith and then my family, and then after that...[golf] is what I love to do."[1] Webb Simpson agrees. "I wasn't born to be a golfer," he says. "I was born to be a child of God."[2]

When my son Stephen was born, I realized I was in danger of stockpiling regrets. For years I had lived for golf. But when I put the game in its rightful spot and gave my clubs a break, a fuller, richer life began. Sure, I experienced withdrawal symptoms at first. Tightness in the chest. Irritability. Gas. But a week later the shakes vanished and perspective arrived.

Pro golfer Bruce Lietzke knows the feeling. When his first child was born, he admitted that golf wasn't even in his top five priorities. At the end of one season Lietzke told his caddie, Al Hansen, that he wouldn't touch his clubs again until the beginning of the next season. Hansen didn't believe him, so he put a banana in Lietzke's golf bag. Lietzke stored the bag in his garage and didn't touch it until January—when he discovered the rotting banana. With these priorities Bruce still managed to rack up 13 wins on the PGA Tour.

I have yet to hear of a man or woman whose last words were, "I just wish I could have golfed one more round." But I've met too many who spent the last half of their lives regretting the first half.

We are all driven by something. The need to drive golf balls. The need for approval. The quest for stuff. But nothing can equal the joy of fulfilling the purpose for which we were created. And nothing can compensate for not discovering it.

Trophy Case

When the president of a large company asked me to relocate to a golfer's paradise and triple my salary, I thought, *I've never heard God speak this clearly before.* But I checked out his offer and soon discovered the job meant "Go Out, Leave Family." Saying no was a turning point in my life. That same day I wrote out my goals:

- Walk closely to Jesus every day.

- Build a strong marriage.

- Love my kids.

- Perform meaningful work.

- Make others homesick for heaven.

Doing this brought me meaning, focus, richness, and a grand sense of purpose.

I still love to hit the links with friends and family, of course. This great game is one of God's gifts to us. But perspective is vital to peace.

Buried deep in my shed is a small box holding an MVP hockey trophy, several small golf and baseball awards, and a tennis medal. A few are broken. Most are rusting. All will decay.

When I stand before God, I will not be asked to divulge my handicap, display those trophies, or prove I had been busy enough. Instead, I will hear God ask, "What did you do with what I gave you? What did you do with my Son?"

Until then the game of golf will be an opportunity, not an obsession.

Now, I'd better go repair that lamp.

Wise are those who find out who will cry at their funeral and then hang out with them.

Tip of the Day: Learn to avoid the ground when teeing off. Jack Nicklaus said, "Through years of experience I have found that air offers less resistance than dirt." If, however, you are trying to claim "The Largest Divot" prize in a tournament, the recommended club is a 6-iron.

3

SAINT MIKE

The best golf partners are those who are just a little worse than
you. Lately I've been getting lots of calls to play with friends.

JAMES ENNS

A part from my children, the person I've golfed with most often
is Mike Olver. Mike is younger than I am, slightly shorter, and
monumentally stronger. He sometimes asks which club I am using
just so he can fall over laughing. On a 150-yard par 3 with nothing
but water between the tee box and the slippery green, Mike chooses
a pitching wedge. I point at some wildlife and pull out an 8-iron,
hoping he doesn't notice.

If I hit the pond, he asks, "What club were you using?"

"Sand wedge," I lie. He just grins.

On most par 4s I use a Big Bertha 1-wood. Mike easily out-drives
me with a 4-iron. One of these days when he isn't looking, I just
might bend that club.

Mike runs a dining hall at Prairie College, and sometimes the
manager at our local golf course asks him to come run the clubhouse to give the staff a break. As often as possible Mike says yes.

Last week when the golf course held its annual bash, Mike was there again. Taking phone calls. Flipping burgers. Listening to golf stories—a big grin all over his face.

There's something you should know about Mike. He takes nothing in return for the work he does at the clubhouse. No money. No bribes. He's over-the-top generous. When patrons hand him a tip, he stuffs the cash in a jar for the employees. He wouldn't want you to know this, but I do. "Why do you do all this for free?" I once asked. He said, "Hey, I'm just a Christian who likes to bless these people. Besides, what do I need? I have a car that runs, a wife who loves me, and a son to golf with." Then he laughed. "Don't you be writing about this. You'll make me sound like a saint."

His eyes got a little misty then, and I knew why. How can a guy so big have a heart so soft? He won't tell you, but he's not writing this book.

One Boy, One Girl

One cloudy day the phone call came. A close friend of Mike's had died of a massive heart attack, leaving a wife and two kids. He had been training for a triathlon. He was 36. The shock hit Mike and his wife hard. Two weeks after the funeral, the Olvers invited the grieving widow and her eight- and ten-year-olds over for dinner.

"My husband was going to take the kids golfing," she said, staring into the distance. "He didn't get..." Her voice trailed off.

Mike and his wife stopped fighting tears and let them go. "I'm so sorry," he said.

"I don't want to be a burden, but would you do something?" she asked. "Would you take them with you sometime when you golf?"

You already know Mike's response. "I'd love to. Do they have clubs?"

"No," she responded. "But I'll look for some."

Last night after Mike finished running things at the golf course, he came by the house to show me something. His face was glowing like polished brass. Seems he was locking up the clubhouse when the manager came over to thank him for filling in. "You know," he said, "you do this for us every year, but you never take a thing in return. Isn't there something we can do for you?"

"Maybe," said Mike. He grinned and pointed to the corner of the pro shop. All evening his eyes had been wandering to two items there, and when he finally had a few spare moments he hurried over to examine them. They were the perfect height. One for a boy. One for a girl. Junior golf bags brimming with drivers, putters, and all the irons, shrink-wrapped in matching black-and-red bags, complete with shoulder straps and kickstands.

"Could you give me a deal on these?" Mike said.

"Take 'em," said the manager.

Mike's grin got wider. "You're kidding."

"Nope. They're yours."

Mike couldn't stop smiling and shaking his head as he told me this. "I'll get some balls and tees and surprise these kids," he said. "And we'll see if we can get their mom lessons so she can take them golfing too."

Mike is one of the strongest men I know. I've played hockey against him, and you can't move this guy from the front of the net without a crane. But true strength has little to do with physical force; it's about gentleness and a servant heart. James 1:27 says, "Pure and genuine religion in the sight of God the Father means caring for orphans and widows in their distress and refusing to let the world corrupt you."

As Saint Mike revved his engine and took off to show the clubs to his wife, I thought, *Some love others out of obligation or for what they can get. Mike loves others because Jesus did. Because they're worth loving.*

Not once since that night have I been tempted to bend this guy's 4-iron.

Heroes are ordinary people who do supernatural things.
Like spreading joy. Like loving others.

Tip of the Day: Davis Love Jr. said, "When it's breezy, hit it easy." It's good advice. Remember the wind is blowing as hard at others as it is at you. Change clubs to keep it low. Keep your balance. Take your time. And remember the three old golfers who were hard of hearing. The first said, "It sure is windy." The second said, "No, it's Thursday." The third said, "Me too. Let's go get a drink."

4

THE BACKYARD CLASSIC

The place of the father in the modern suburban family
is a very small one, particularly if he plays golf.

BERTRAND RUSSELL

When we were first married, cash was scarce. The banker asked if we had some. We said, "Not much." He asked if we'd like a joint account. Ramona said no. She would prefer to open one with someone who had money. Despite our lack of cash, those were years rich in memories, relationships, and fun. When dinner out was impossible, we had picnics on the kitchen floor. When a round at Pebble Beach was unthinkable, I turned to my neighbor to the south. He could build anything.

In the hands of Vance, salvaged junk morphed into bookshelves. Discarded maple became a handsome porch swing. From garbage bags and duct tape came waterslides our kids would talk about for years. Vance even built a jungle gym out of power poles. I still don't know where he got them, but our power was a little intermittent after that.

Upon finishing the towering edifice, Vance informed me there was ample leftover wood. "We'll build an elevated green in the vacant field behind our houses."

Thus was birthed the Airport Golf and Country Club, so christened for the abandoned airplane hangar that dominated the south end of all 18 fairways.

Early the next morning we mowed the field with Vance's lawnmower. We raised the blade high enough to avoid a thousand rocks culled from our gardens through the years. And soon the contoured fairways rivalled the rough at Pine Valley. "Winter rules," we agreed.

The AGCC was unique in that it had 18 fairways but only one green. The holes were determined by creating varying tee box locations throughout the neighborhood and sinking soup cans into the massive elevated sand green. The hangar would serve a dual purpose: 1) to provide a solid backstop to keep our errant drives from decapitating pedestrians on the sidewalk that ran along holes nine and eighteen, and 2) to afford shade from the hot sun so we could practice on the green—or the brown, as we came to call it. When the sun set, we surveyed our work and saw that it was good. "Be up by nine." Vance smiled, cracking his knuckles. "I think we can get you on."

With dawn came the realization that there was more work to be done, so we manicured the course, flinging rocks from fairways and yanking weeds from the green. And in the late afternoon the Airport Classic finally began.

Nearby our wives tended hot dogs over a fire pit full of glowing embers. Amid five half-dead pines dubbed Sherwood Forest, our children launched pine cones at imaginary targets, and all was well with the world.

The first tee was nestled smack-dab in the center of my backyard. "Replace your divots," my wife reminded us. And we did, of course. Hole one was a sharp dogleg to the left. The smaller children vacated the swing set as we took aim. Hole two was a straight shot from Vance's backyard, a lob wedge over the raspberries and across the pea patch. Number three we nicknamed "Doo Doo." It required splitting two tall spruce trees with a sand wedge, through a thicket of dense lilac bushes, all from a neighbor's doggy minefield. To this day it is one of the most challenging holes I've ever tiptoed through.

After three holes we broke for hot dogs and juicy stories from the children's adventures. After supper they climbed the trees to watch as we completed our spirited game, culminating with a winner-take-the-rest-of-the-hot-dogs playoff on eighteen, the longest hole. The tee box was recessed and lay far beyond Sherwood Forest across the road on Larry McClanahan's front lawn. From there you had to clear Larry's car, then the road, then the five-tree forest and a grove of maple trees. Larry watched from the window, his fingers crossed.

Hitting and sticking the sand brown off the tee was an automatic hole in one. We never came close. As I think about it now, I realize I'd pay a handsome sum to go back and try again.

A few days ago I walked through that neighborhood again. The ancient hangar is gone. The fairways have grown over. The yards are about the same, but there are fewer divots, to be sure.

Since that time I've had opportunities to golf some magnificent courses from Seattle to Singapore, but few memories are as sweet as that of the Airport Classic. Time spent with a good friend while our wives manned the fire and the gallery of tired children peeked out of Sherwood to cheer our loud rebounds off that hangar wall. Life was simpler then. Sometimes we're far richer than we think.

A simple life is a full life.

> **Tip of the Day:** When you're playing for a score, go with the club that works. I once birdied a par 5 using only a 7-iron. Be warned though. When putting with a 7-iron, it is often necessary to block out the scorn and the derision of your playing partners.

5

MICKEY'S LAST HOMER

He who has the fastest golf cart never has a bad lie.

MICKEY MANTLE

*If you read history you will find that the Christians
who did most for the present world were precisely
those who thought most of the next.*

C.S. LEWIS

I n the world of sports, my first love is golf, followed by baseball. Baseball players love golf. Hank Aaron said, "It took me 17 years to get 3,000 hits in baseball. I did it in one afternoon on the golf course." Ball players are also notorious pranksters, and few were more accomplished at pranks than Billy Martin, second baseman and five-time manager of the New York Yankees. His teammate, Hall-of-Famer Mickey Mantle, was often his victim.

So Mickey thought long and hard on ways to pay Billy back. One day the two went hunting on land owned by a friend. Arriving at the farm, Mickey told Billy to sit tight while he asked the farmer for permission to hunt on his property. The farmer graciously agreed, but asked Mickey for a favor. "I have a mule. It's old and sick. I need to put it down, but I can't bring myself to do it. Would you?"

"No," said Mickey, but the friend was persistent. "Please. I love this mule. It would mean a lot to me." And so finally Mickey said yes. As he returned to the pickup, an idea hit him between the ears. He tried to keep a straight face as he told Billy, "He won't let us hunt! We've wasted a three-hour trip! Some friend he is! I'll show him!"

With that, Mickey Mantle grabbed his rifle, stomped off toward the barn, and shot the mule dead.

Suddenly he heard more shots from behind him and ran toward the sound. There stood Billy Martin, motioning frantically. "I shot two of his cows!" he yelled. "Jump in! Let's go!"

I am happy to inform you the story isn't true. Though one Yankee credited Mickey with telling it first, it's an urban legend that's been passed along through the years.

Now the Good News

My favorite Mickey Mantle story *is* true, however. It was told at his funeral by teammate Bobby Richardson, the Yankee second baseman during that wild era.

Bobby began his speech with hilarious stories of Mickey's shenanigans. Then he got serious. "Mickey was always laughing," he said, "but underneath it all there was a fear of death he tried to cover and fill." Though loved by the world, he had lived a hard life. His wife and sons were all treated for alcoholism and begged him to do the same. The doctor told Mantle that 40 years of drinking had damaged his liver so badly that "it looked like a doorstop...Your next drink could be your last."

Before the final game Bobby and Mickey played together, Richardson invited a Christian friend to talk to the Yankees. The friend told them the Bible says three things: (1) there's a problem and the problem is sin, (2) the answer to the problem is Jesus, and (3) the Bible demands a decision. Then he wrote on a blackboard, "What have you done with Jesus Christ?"

Years later, Mickey Mantle phoned Bobby, asking if he would pray with him. Bobby did and then repeated Philippians 4:7, inviting Mickey to cast all his cares upon the Lord: "And the peace of God, which transcends all understanding, will guard your hearts and your minds in Christ Jesus" (NIV).

More years passed. One day Bobby received a call from the Mantle family. Mickey was dying. Would Bobby come for a final visit and then stay and speak at the funeral? When Richardson arrived at the hospital he found Mickey Mantle's face shining with joy. Mickey had once said, "It was all I lived for, to play baseball." But he'd found a greater purpose. He said, "I've been wanting to tell you something. I've received Christ as my Savior."

When Bobby's wife arrived later, she said, "Mickey, if you were standing before God and he asked, 'Why should I let you in my heaven?' what would you say?" Quick as a flash Mickey answered, "'For God so loved the world that He gave His only begotten Son, that whoever believes in Him should not perish but have everlasting life.'"[1]

At the funeral, Bobby Richardson told the church packed with baseball celebrities and media, "If Mick could hold a press conference from where he is today, I know he would introduce you to his true hero. The one who died in his place to give him everlasting life, his Savior, Jesus Christ. And the greatest tribute that you could give Mickey today would be for you to receive his Savior too."[2]

Mickey famously said, "If I'd known I was going to live this long, I'd have taken better care of myself." How good to know that in the end, God took good care of Mickey, redeemed him, and welcomed him into heaven.

In the end, perhaps life is a lot like baseball. The whole point of the thing is to go home.

Believe in heaven and you run toward life, not away from it.

> **Tip of the Day:** Chip the ball when the lie is poor, the green is hard, and you've had a bad day. Pitch the ball when the lie is good, the green is soft, and all is well with the world. If you don't know the difference between a chip and a pitch, just hit the thing.

6

THE ELUSIVE HOLE IN ONE

Golf is not a game of great shots. It's a game of the best misses. The people who win make the smallest mistakes.

GENE LITTLER, FORMER PGA TOUR PLAYER

Most tournaments I am privileged to attend offer prizes ranging from hats that don't fit to clubs I can't hit to new cars I can't win. My favorite hole is always the short par 3 offering a Caribbean cruise for eight or a covetable Jeep Cherokee if I simply unleash the perfect shot. I know the odds of an amateur hitting an ace are roughly 1 in 13,000, but still I dream. I know I've a better chance of hitting a striped kangaroo off the tee, but still I hope.

Three friends were witnesses on the day I teed up on a meticulously groomed course called the Bear—designed by the Golden Bruin himself, Jack Nicklaus. As I stood on that par 3 coveting a $10,000 prize, I thought, *I could give this money to needy children. My children.*

To claim the prize, my ball would have to carry over a lake, land on the front of the green, and jam on the brakes 190 yards away. It would require a long iron, a stiff tailwind, and a miracle not unlike the parting of the Red Sea. And so I bargained with God. "Lord, first of all, help me not miss the ball like I did on the last tee. And if it's not too much to ask, strengthen my feeble arms and help this little white thing drop into the cup. And when it does, I promise to give you...um...11 percent. No, make that 12."

I had bounced shots onto the green using carts, trees, water hazards, and ball washers. I had come within six inches of making a hole in one on our home course before telling a friend I was glad to have missed. Why? Because our course has an annoying custom written by someone who has clearly never hit a hole in one: the acer buys drinks for everyone in the clubhouse, including people who drove out to the course when they heard what you did. This is like celebrating Father's Day by making Dad bring the whole family breakfast in bed.

All this to say, I had yet to hit a hole in one.

And then I stepped up to the fourteenth tee with sins forgiven, gladness in my heart, and a 4-iron in my hands. I cleaned the grooves in that club with a tee. I scrubbed a blade of grass from the ball. I prayed a biblical prayer for a straight path, for God's leading beside still waters, for a tiny miracle to take place.

Then I took a swing.

My release was enviable, my follow-through picture-perfect. We watched in awe as the ball took off. It accelerated as it rose, traversing the lake and continuing to climb. It descended exquisitely as if it were a tiny radio-controlled drone, honing in on the flagstick, causing my heart to thump in wild anticipation.

The lady there to witness such events arose from her cart. She danced the polka for about two seconds and buried her face in her hands. Was it from grief or glee?

Arriving at the hole, we surveyed the carnage. The ball had left its mark one dreadful foot before the pin and somehow rolled straight over the hole, coming to rest 18 awful inches behind the cup. I asked the judge if I didn't at least get something, you know, a consolation prize. Maybe just $4,000, or a hat. She said no. Close only counts in lawn darts.

"Come on, God," I said as I tapped the stubborn ball into the hole. "Was it too much to ask?" I should have known.

Billy Graham said, "The one time my prayers are never answered is on the golf course." Until then, I thought he was joking.

Miracle at Sea

I'm sure you have never treated God like a vending machine, but sometimes I do. A little girl prayed, "God, please change the taste of asparagus. Thanks." I'm sure God smiled, but I've tasted asparagus. God's answer was no. Sometimes his answer is wait. Sometimes it's yes. And sometimes I think he says yes with a mischievous smile.

During a transatlantic voyage, the captain of an ocean liner asked the celebrated preacher F.B. Meyer to address the first-class passengers on the topic of "Answered Prayer." An agnostic listening told a friend, "I didn't believe a word of it." Still, when he heard Meyers was scheduled to speak again, the agnostic decided to return to hear him. But first he popped two oranges in his pockets for a snack.

Walking through third class, he saw an elderly woman asleep in her deck chair, her hands open. He grinned and laid the oranges in her outstretched palms. After the meeting, he found her eating one of them.

"Is it good?" he said.

"Yes, sir," she replied. "My Father is very good."

"Your father is still alive?" he asked.

"Yes. I've been seasick for days. So I asked God to send me an orange. I woke and found he'd sent me two." That day the agnostic put his faith in Jesus.

My Prayer Today

I did not pray for a hole in one today. I did not pray to win. I prayed for others who have it worse than I do. I thanked God for life and health and redemption and people whose love and forgiveness startles me. I thanked God that he knows my needs and has never once stopped meeting them. And I told him that if ever he should allow me a hole in one, I would be grateful for that too.

God always gives us what we pray for. Or something better.

> **Tip of the Day:** To hit a fade, align your clubface to the target and then align your feet and shoulders so they are slightly open (facing to the left for right-handed golfers). Then swing normally. To top the ball, choke up on your club and lift your head.

7

ESCAPE FROM THE HANOI HILTON

I want the same discipline in my faith that I have in my golf game.
SCOTT SIMPSON

*Success in this game depends less on strength of
body than strength of mind and character.*
ARNOLD PALMER

Colonel George Hall, US Air Force pilot, was flying reconnaissance over North Vietnam when his world exploded. Struck by ground fire, his jet burst into flames. Hall ejected and parachuted to the ground, where Vietcong guerillas captured and incarcerated him as a POW at the infamous Hanoi Hilton. It was September 27, 1965.

Interrogated and tortured, he endured near starvation and solitary confinement—sometimes for months in a row. To stay sane, Hall hid a stick in his tiny cell. He had an idea. While others gave in to despair, he would turn his confinement zone into a practice field. As a scratch golfer and captain of the US Naval Academy golf team, he would develop a virtual golf course in his mind—18 holes that beckoned him to some faraway place where he could play the game he loved.

Each day Colonel Hall awoke looking forward to the day's round. He pulled on an imaginary collared shirt, golf socks, pants, and shoes. He topped it all off by donning an imaginary golf cap, hoisting an imaginary bag to his shoulders, and heading to "the course." There he dealt with those first tee jitters, calmed his nerves on the tee box, and selected the correct club. He stood behind the ball for alignment, went through his customary setup routine, used his left thumb to represent the handle of the club, and placed his right hand around the thumb. Then he raised that stick to the apex of his swing and brought it through, holding his photo finish position, knowing from experience where the ball had gone.

"I'd play at least nine holes every day," he said. "I'd visualize a golf course I had played and enjoyed. I'd hit every shot with that stick, and then I'd walk around that room. For instance, I'd hit my driver and then step off 240 yards or so around the room. I'd think about how long the hole was and decide what club to hit next. I not only walked from the tee to the green but from the green to the next tee. I'd talk to people I imagined I was playing with."

Colonel Hall never pretended he was squaring off against Arnold Palmer or Jack Nicklaus. Just friends. He never imagined making birdies or eagles. Just pars. "A pleasant round of golf, that's all I wanted."

Guards watching must have considered him certifiably insane— that crazy prisoner who swings an old stick and talks to imaginary people. He's lost his mind.

But the opposite was true.

Sometimes he was playing his home course. Always he was picturing the wonder of the fairways around him, savoring the sounds of the birds, the wind, the club striking the ball. Sometimes the fairways weren't fair, the greens too fast, the rough too high. Always he made necessary adjustments. After each hole, Hall licked his imaginary pencil and wrote down his score.

In life and golf, success is won or lost on the battlefield of the mind.

Unsung Moments

I sometimes wonder what Paul of Tarsus, who persecuted Christians before becoming one, did when Governor Felix plunked him in prison for two years.[1] Unlike his friend Peter, Paul experienced no earth-shattering deliverance. No miracles. Just life behind bars.

Paul was no stranger to prison. He wrote letters while in chains, often using sports terms. "Run to win!" "Take a new grip with your tired hands." Perhaps he hoisted an imaginary club or bounced an imaginary ball. We don't know. But we do know that Paul turned his confinement zone into a practice field. He celebrated communion, gave thanks, cared for other prisoners, proclaimed good news, fasted, prayed, and trusted God. "Let us run with perseverance the race marked out for us," he later wrote, "fixing our eyes on Jesus, the pioneer and perfecter of faith."[2]

Any admired athlete or effective leader is king or queen of unsung moments. Moments no one knows about. Times of repeating fundamentals, developing muscle memory, winning the battle of the mind.

Sometimes God's work in us requires long stretches of the mundane, slogging through routines. At times our plans grind to a stifling halt, and we are tempted to believe that God is busy elsewhere. Will we quit or faithfully practice for that moment when our time comes? For Paul, all that prison practice paid off. When he was released, he helped turn the world right side up.

The Payoff

On February 12, 1973, after seven years, four months, and eighteen days (he kept track) in a seven-by-seven-foot cell, Colonel Hall finally checked out of the Hanoi Hilton. Back home, he settled quickly into life with his wife, Patsy, and their children. And he couldn't wait to play golf.

Six weeks later he was invited to play in the Greater New Orleans POW Pro-Am Open, where he found himself on one of golf's grandest stages.

Some remember that Jack Nicklaus won that 1973 Open. Others remember an even greater victory. They remember Colonel George Hall and the smile on his face. They remember how thin he looked. He had lost 100 pounds on a daily ration of 300 calories. And they remember his miraculous score. George hadn't touched a golf club in seven years. Yet he shot his handicap—a 76.

Discipline is painful. But not as painful as regret.

> **Tip of the Day:** There are no shortcuts through the fields of discipline and practice. So have fun with it. On the range, visualize a hole that gives you trouble, then "play" it. At the office, keep a stick with you and play an imaginary round in honor of Colonel Hall.

8

BUILDING THE PERFECT CLUB

*My greatest fear is that he'll die before I
do. What will I do with all this stuff?*

SHARON MATES, WIFE OF BARRY MATES, WHOSE GOLF BALL COLLECTION INCLUDES
50,000 BALLS FROM ALL OVER THE WORLD

*If we let culture happen to us, we'll end up fat, addicted,
broke, with a house full of junk and no time.*

MARY PIPHER, PSYCHOLOGIST

Without a doubt, the most easygoing golfer I know is Jason Miller. A father of five, Jason routinely shoots well past 100, and that's just on the fourth hole. The funny thing is, he does so with a grin. Perhaps it comes from knowing he has a few hours of unbroken silence away from his five children. But I think it may have more to do with the fact that Jason has learned to golf light.

Apart from the app he uses to keep score, Jason keeps it simple. He doesn't own a golf bag, preferring instead to clutch five clubs in one hand: a driver, a 5-wood, two rusted mid-irons, and a bent putter. Jason's pockets bulge with golf balls, and when he runs out, he simply strolls along the edge of the creek, parting grass and saying, "Come on home to Papa."

Standard wear for Jason is shorts, a collared shirt, and golf sandals, which he discards when entering the creek. "I can feel the balls better this way," is how he explains it.

Jason's unencumbered style gave me the idea of walking the course with just a 6-iron and a putter, scratching my head trying to figure out why I shot roughly the same score as I do lugging the full set. An old guy saw me carrying two clubs and wandered over. "You don't need two," he said. "Here's the only club you'll ever need." He pulled a clever little creation from his bag. The toe boasted a spring-loaded screw allowing you to adjust the clubface trajectory from sand wedge to putter.

"Mind if I give it a try?" I said.

"Knock yourself out," he said.

And I almost did. My shot careened off the screw-heavy toe, causing ducks to scatter. This club was the single worst golf invention since someone decided to shrink the cup to four inches.

"Forty bucks and it's yours," he said, oblivious to the scattering ducks.

I thought to myself, *Is there a sport with more stuff?*

Golf now has the Swing Shirt. It looks like a straitjacket. You insert your arms through a snug-fitting center sleeve and your swing is fixed. Or you can just buy a roll of duct tape and have a friend wrap you up.

And there's the Ghost Putter, which appears to be wielded by...well, a ghost. It stands on its own so that you can stand behind it for a better line. Sadly, you still have to hit the ball for yourself.

One day as we golfed, Jason and I talked about inventing the perfect club.

It would include a tiny, built-in weed whacker activated by a button on the grip. A ball in the rough? Simply flip the switch and clear away the offending grass. A second button would engage a high-powered blower for those putts that just won't drop. They say 80 percent of short putts don't go in. Now 100 percent would. Just press a button and blow the ball into the hole. It would have a reverse switch too, of course, for bunker shots. Hit a trap? Not a problem. Just flip a vacuum switch.

Jason took another swipe at the ball and walked toward the creek. I shouldered my bag and trudged along beside him. "I went to my high school reunion this summer," he said. "Forty people my age. All they talked about were the houses they were building or the stuff they owned."

Setting down my bag, I studied it. The bag had all the clubs. Plus an umbrella, a retractable club brush, and enough snacks to feed a Boy Scout troop. One can't be overprepared, so I carry bug spray, sunscreen, a hand warmer, rain gear, a beanie, extra socks, and a jacket. I have blister tape, Band-Aids, aspirin, and lip balm. There's a towel, divot and ball mark tools, two water bottles, a Sharpie, and more coins and pencils than you'll find in a kitchen drawer.

Call me crazy, but I'm not alone. We all get side-tracked by stuff. We all shoulder things we're not meant to carry. Anxiety. Worry. Fear. Excess stress. Things that suck away the joy God intended us to experience.

The Right Stuff

I told Jason about flying into a beautiful city, looking down and admiring the golf courses, marveling at the size of the houses. Thinking about how we're buying stuff we don't need with money we don't have to impress people we don't like so we can get air miles we're too busy to use. How we have clocks to shine the time on our ceilings and cell phones that work underwater. I looked at Jason, standing there holding his clubs and his shoes, and realized we all carry so much more stuff than we need.

"Thanks, man," I said. "I needed a reminder that all these things don't matter, to slow down and enjoy this game."

Some call this approach to life simple, but simplicity is not simplemindedness. The people I admire most are those who live light. Who recognize things for what they are—goods to enhance life, not to weigh us down.

And so, amid historically unprecedented affluence, we are wise to walk unencumbered. Buying less. Giving more. Recognizing that everything we have is a gift from God.

I tried to give my bag to Jason. He wouldn't take it. Too bad. There's enough stuff in there to take care of his family for weeks. So I'll give it to one of my kids. And tell them the last check I write is going to be to the undertaker. And it's gonna bounce.

Even ants have time to attend a picnic.

> **Tip of the Day:** To increase your distance off the tee, warm up and stretch before you play. For $20 you can buy exercise tubing and practice your swing with resistance. Tuck your right hand beneath your left. Gently apply pressure from the back of your right hand against your left as you slowly pull your upper body into your backswing. Hold 15 seconds and repeat. Actually hitting the ball farther will require a club.

9

GOLFING WITH MY WIFE

Give me golf clubs, fresh air, and a beautiful partner,
and you can keep the clubs and the fresh air.

JACK BENNY

Marriage counselors claim there are three activities that will tax a good marriage: 1) building a house, 2) wallpapering, and 3) golfing together. Okay, I'm making the last one up. But the truth is, Ramona and I have done all three. House building was a breeze. Wallpapering was a cinch. But golfing?

I'm not sure what it is about this magnificent game that brings out the impatience in me, but I must hurry up and find out.

I have been a sought-after coach in two sports. I have given my wife free lessons on stance, swing, and follow-through. She has fine clubs and a sweet swing. But she lacks one thing: hope. Hope that the next shot will go farther and straighter. That on the next shot something good will happen. Where would the golfer be without hope?

One Tuesday evening we tackled the course together. I cheered her on—even when she topped the ball, causing gophers to scatter. On the third hole I said, "Let me show you something," and proceeded to lace a perfect tee shot down the fairway. I turned as if to say, "See, darlin', that's how it's done." But she'd missed the whole beautiful thing. She was pointing to her right as a great blue heron used the creek for a runway. I said something so dumb then that I surprised us both. "Come on. We're here to golf, not to enjoy ourselves."

Thankfully, she began to laugh. And I did too. Her laugh has been a gift to our marriage the last few decades.

The Walk

Ramona teed up her pink ball and then thought better of it. Cramming it back into her pocket, she took my hand and said, "I'll just walk with you."

We were all of 16 when our walk together began. That was the year she told me about Huntington's Disease. How she had a 50/50 chance of dying from this genetic disorder. A decade later we discovered she didn't have it, but her brother Dennis did. He passed away after being curled up in a fetal position for ten years. Two sisters were in nursing homes now, their bodies and minds changed by this dreadful disease.

I shook my head as we walked. That morning we'd received an email from a nephew informing us that Ramona's sister Miriam had been hospitalized for good.

During the past eight months her deterioration had accelerated to the point where there were times she didn't recognize her own children. After seeing a recent CT scan, doctors remarked that they couldn't believe Miriam could still walk and carry on a conversation. Due to pure determination and will, she had been able to keep doing some of the things that were important to her. But after ten years of patiently caring for her night and day, Miriam's husband, Jim, was left with no alternative other than to put her trustingly into the care of others.

"Life is falling apart at the edges, but not at the core," she told a doctor. "At the core, I know I'm loved by God and promised the eternal joys of heaven." Both Jim's and Miriam's attitudes in the face of overwhelming obstacles have been a testimony of God's grace from the day she was diagnosed. This note from her son David following her move into long-term care gives you a glimpse of her character: "It doesn't seem to bother her that she is not at home anymore. As long as she knows where her bed is, that there will be food for breakfast (especially for all the others), and that she gets her Frappuccino, she's happy." He drew a huge smiley face after these words.

The Storm

In the midst of this valley, Jim and Miriam have shown their children and hundreds of others that one of the keys to a joy-filled life is allowing adversity to forge us—to bring us together, not tear us apart. When I think of patience and perseverance, I think of these two shining examples.

A few years ago, at a family reunion, Jim and I attempted to golf together. The weather was dreadful. Horizontal rain stabbed us from the north and dark clouds threatened us with lightning bolts. We ended up putting for a few minutes on the practice green before quickly retreating from the storm.

How thankful I am that Jim did not retreat from the most major storm of his life. How thankful I am for the example of this saint of a man—one of my heroes.

Thinking of Miriam and Jim while playing golf with my wife changed everything. I would be a fool not to be grateful for her health and for each and every day we have together. I would be a fool not to put away the instructions, laugh more, and say "good shot" every chance I get. In fact, since I began saying such things, roughly 112 times on nine holes, I've noticed she's enjoying the game a whole lot more.

That Tuesday night, as the sun dipped behind the ninth green and the sprinklers began their rhythmic *chut chut*, we sat on the clubhouse veranda sipping lemonade. "Will you still love me when I'm old?" I asked. She grinned and said, "I already do."

We got to talking of life and marriage and things we'd like to do more of if God allows us to grow even older together. It wasn't anywhere near the top of her list, but I was surprised when she mentioned golf. "Wanna come out here again next week?" I asked. She laughed and said, "Sure, but first you need to help me hang some wallpaper."

You will never master golf or marriage. But you can learn to put bad shots behind you and celebrate the good.

> **Tip of the Day:** The absolute best golf tip I can offer a young person is this: find a great partner and marry well like I did. God bless you, Ramona.

10

THE SPARK OF FAILURE

I have a tip that can take five strokes off
anyone's game. It's called an eraser.

ARNOLD PALMER

Courage is going from failure to failure without losing enthusiasm.

WINSTON CHURCHILL

One of my favorite golf movies is *Bobby Jones: Stroke of Genius.* When a man asks his Scottish caddy what he can do to improve his game, the caddy says, "Stop playing for two weeks and then give it up altogether."

We've all felt like quitting, haven't we? In golf. In life.

Last year the highest-earning deceased celebrities were Michael Jackson ($400 million), Elvis ($40 million), and Arnold Palmer ($35 million), followed closely by another golf enthusiast.

Early in life his friends called him Sparky, though he hated the nickname. Sparky failed every subject in eighth grade and still holds the record for being the worst physics student in the school's history. In high school he flunked physics, Latin, algebra, English, and

Relationships 101. If a classmate said hello outside of school, he was surprised. If a girl looked his way, he was shocked. Sparky never dated or even asked a girl out. He'd dealt with enough failure in his life. Why risk being turned down again?

At the age of 15, however, he began to excel at golf. He became a caddy, eventually claiming a trophy as St. Paul, Minnesota, caddy champion. By 17, Sparky was a 2-handicapper, building his game around a deadly accurate power fade off the tee. But one dreadful day Sparky's poor play cost his school golf team the championship.

He turned his attention to drawing cartoons but found that no one shared his enthusiasm for his characters. Even the school yearbook committee turned him down. After graduation, he sent the Walt Disney Studios samples of his artwork and once again was rejected.

Sparky began to realize his life resembled a cartoon strip. He decided to tell his own story in cartoons—a childhood full of the misadventures of a little boy loser, a chronic underachiever, a cartoon character who would be loved the world over as Charlie Brown.

Charles Schulz's *Peanuts* characters often mirrored his passions for golf. Schroeder was even named after a caddy friend. In one cartoon, Charlie Brown is talking to Snoopy. "Tournament golf can be very nerve-wracking," he tells the little dog. "Do you get nervous when you're on the first tee?" "I don't know," responds Snoopy, shaking violently. "I've never made it to the first tee."

Charles Schulz didn't just make it to the first tee. He kept teeing it up well into his seventies.

He often played twice a week, mostly at Oakmont Golf Club in Santa Rosa, California, one of five Sonoma County courses where he was an honorary member. A fixture at the AT&T Pebble Beach National Pro-Am, Schulz was always mindful of the rules and was called "a tough competitor" by *Golf Digest*. One weekend he flew in two foursomes for a game of golf at Pebble Beach. On the way home he reminded one of his friends that he been shorted 50 cents on a bet.

In interviews, he let it be known that the thoughts expressed in the strip reflected his own hopes, fears, and faith. Schulz grew up in a Lutheran home, joined the Church of God as an adult, and taught a Sunday school class. He regularly injected biblical ideas, quotes from the Bible, and theological values into his strip.

"Sparky was very honorable to the game," said longtime friend and Oakmont director of Golf Dean James, when Schulz passed away at the age of 77. *Golf Digest* called Schulz "Golf's good man."

In her book *Good Grief: The Story of Charles M. Schulz*, Rheta Grimsley Johnson wrote, "Rejection is his specialty, losing his area of expertise. He has spent a lifetime perfecting failure."[1]

I cannot think of Charles Schulz without thinking of a host of Bible characters who "perfected" failure. If anyone had the yips, it was Moses. Yet God helped him face his fear and lead the Israelites out of captivity in Egypt. David was guilty of adultery and murder. Still, he was called a man after God's own heart. Jonah ran from God until he was down in the mouth. After a whale of a tale, God used him to turn the hearts of an entire city heavenward. Each of these men discovered what to do with failure. They knew it isn't falling down that makes you a failure. It's claiming someone pushed you. They knew that failure doesn't come in the falling. It comes in not getting back up.

With God's help, your greatest achievement may be just beyond your greatest failure.

Failure is a chance to start over, wiser than before.

Tip of the Day: If you allow for a slice, you'll get one. Concentrate on what it takes to hit the ball squarely. Famed golf instructor Harvey Penick advised us to "pretend you are on a baseball field at home plate...Aim your body slightly to the right of second base, but aim your clubface straight at the base. Then hit the ball over the shortstop. Use a 7-iron at first, then a 3-wood."[2] Work on your slice until you can hook the ball.

11

I'M NUMBER THREE

*There is one thing in this world that is dumber than playing
golf. That is watching someone else playing golf. What do
you actually get to see? Thirty-seven guys in polyester slacks
squinting at the sun. Doesn't that set your blood racing?*

PETER ANDREWS, SPORTSWRITER

My library consists almost entirely of borrowed books. One of my favorites is jam-packed with random quotes from the wild world of sports. Like this from Hall of Fame catcher Johnny Bench: "I was thinking about making a comeback, until I pulled a muscle vacuuming."

Heavyweight legend Rocky Graziano uttered one of the best one-liners ever when he said, "I quit school in the sixth grade because of pneumonia. Not because I had it, but because I couldn't spell it."

NBA executive Pat Williams said, "We can't win at home. We can't win on the road. I just can't figure out where else to play."

"If I had my way," wrote the humorist H.L. Mencken, "any man guilty of golf would be ineligible for any office of trust in the United States."

NBA center Chuck Nevitt said, "My sister's expecting a baby, and I don't know if I'm going to be an uncle or an aunt."

The press couldn't go to print fast enough when former Hall of Fame NFL receiver Jerry Rice said, "I feel like I'm the best, but you're not going to get me to say that."

We would all like to be the best, I suppose. To hold the trophy high and chant, "I'm number one!" Most of my sports career was spent shouting, "I'm number 12," which is not something you shout loudly. The truth is, no matter how low my handicap or how high my rank, I'm not number one. Those who follow Jesus believe that God comes first, others next, then us.

When you suddenly awake thunderstruck, realizing you're more concerned with giving than receiving, you have unearthed gold. You have discovered the greatest key to lasting friendship: *selflessness*.

Improving Your Serve

I've golfed with some mighty fine pros, but two of the worst golfers on the planet left the most lasting of impressions on me. My brothers-in-law, Bill and Jim, have faithfully nursed their wives through one of earth's most merciless diseases, Huntington's.

Like my sisters-in-law, David Ireland was dying from a crippling neurological disease. His wife was expecting when he wrote the book *Letters to an Unborn Child*. David would never show that child how to hold a golf club or throw a baseball, and he would never hear David say the words "I love you, son," but that child would see true love in action.

Here's what David told his child about his wife.

> Your mother is very special. [Taking her] out to din-
> ner...means she has to dress me, shave me, brush my
> teeth, comb my hair; wheel me out of the house and
> down the steps, open the garage and put me in the car,

take the pedals off the chair, stand me up, sit me in the seat of the car, twist me around so that I'm comfortable, fold the wheelchair, put it in the car, go around to the other side of the car, start it up, back it out, get out of the car, pull the garage door down, get back into the car, and drive off to the restaurant. And then, it starts all over again...[Finally] we sit down to...dinner, and she feeds me throughout the entire meal. And when it's over she pays the bill, pushes the wheelchair out to the car again, and reverses the same routine. And...with real warmth she'll say, "Honey, thank you for taking me out to dinner." I never quite know what to answer.

[When] I have to wash my hair; this involves sitting with my shirt off in front of the sink. There's a mirror there and I am able to look at myself...the muscles and flesh...having slowly disappeared...[and] I begin to feel depressed...Joyce will say, "Oh, don't look! I'm going to take that silly mirror down if you don't stop admiring yourself."

Then...your mother will sit down...place my hand in her lap and...say, "You're so handsome to me. You're the most handsome man in the world. I love you so much." And somehow, out of the ancient well of our experience together, I know she means it.[1]

We need to hear about such people, don't we? I admire the skills of athletes, but we must never elevate the stars above the servants. Huntington's is perhaps the last disease I would have chosen for our family. Its goodbye is among the longest and most agonizing. Yet through it I have met the most compassionate and selfless people, saints who are like David. Such sacrificial love is the cornerstone of true joy, happiness, and faith itself.

"Improving your serve" is a tennis term, I know, but it's for the rest of us too. There is no higher calling. Philippians 2:3-4 tells us, "Don't be selfish...Be humble, thinking of others as better than yourselves. Don't look out only for your own interests, but take an interest in others, too."

We're on the pathway to joy when we smile and say, "I'm number three."

The world crowns success; God crowns faithfulness.

Tip of the Day: The best club you'll ever own is a good attitude. Play one shot at a time. Start again on the next hole. If this doesn't work and you have hit more than 18 shots on the first hole, or hit more than one person, talk to the course marshal. Sometimes they'll let you start again.

12

FORE IS SHORT FOR FORGIVENESS

*The reason the pro tells you to keep your head
down is so you can't see him laughing.*

PHYLLIS DILLER

*Never break your putter and your driver
in the same round or you're dead.*

TOMMY BOLT

My son Jeffrey almost killed someone recently. It's not something we mention around the house. In fact, until now only a handful of people knew about it.

Our round that day began with such promise. The first tee box always summons us with the opportunity to start again—a topic my son and I would talk about for weeks to come.

Hole one is a scant 330 yards from the tee box and something my son, the young gun, can't resist. Jeffrey had a new driver with a head like a waffle iron. Carefully placing a brand-new ball on a brand-new tee, he stood back, took a few perfect practice swings, and then smacked his first shot. Hard.

To say he hooked the shot is like saying the Sahara Desert contains sand.

A fellow club member was enjoying his round at the time. He was standing on the second green 90 yards away lining up a long putt and thinking pleasant thoughts when he heard two guys yelling, "Fore!" at roughly the same decibel level as music in a teenager's earbuds.

Unfortunately, he barely had time to blink before the ball struck him hard on the thigh. The poor guy went down like a blindsided boxer. I thought he was dead. *He* thought he was dead. Running toward him as fast as we could run in golf shoes, we wondered if we should call an ambulance or a hearse.

Thank God he was all right.

The evening after The Incident we rang the man's doorbell, and the poor guy stood there holding a bag of ice as we apologized for the eleventh time.

"No problem," he said at last. "I'm a welder. I'm used to incoming objects. Would you like to see the bruise?"

Why, yes, we would. We're guys. We winced. It was the size of a grapefruit. Discolored. With dimples. We handed him a card and a gift. In turn, he offered my son as great a gift as Jeffrey could have hoped for.

"I forgive you," he said.

A Tale of Two Drivers

At the back of a church where I was speaking, I asked a former Buddhist what he saw in Christ that he never saw in Buddha. He didn't pause to think about it. "Forgiveness for my sin," he said. He didn't stop there. "The Bible says that if we confess our sin God is faithful and just to forgive us and to cleanse us too."

Years ago, a story of forgiveness unfolded during the British

Open. Though Ian Woosnam was ranked number one that year, had his own jet airplane, and owned a home with a putting green, he had been on a "downhill slide," according to the media. But here he was atop the leader board again. On the last day of the tournament, he was tied with four other golfers. At only five feet four inches, Woosnam was poised to stand tall in the winner's circle.

After nearly acing a hole, he found himself leading the final round. Bending over to tee up his ball, he turned to caddie Miles Byrne for a club.

Instead, he got the shock of his golf career.

"You're going to go ballistic," Byrne told him.

"Why?" asked Woosnam.

"We've got two drivers in the bag."

Woosnam knew immediately what that meant. He had 13 other clubs. With two drivers, that made 15. Only 14 are allowed. Woosnam had to call a two-stroke penalty on himself. A penalty that would knock him out of the lead.

"At that moment, I felt like I had been kicked in the teeth," Woosnam later said.

When the day was over, he had fallen four strokes short of the winning score posted by David Duvall and was left wondering what might have been had one of the worst gaffs in major championship history not occurred.

The real story, however, came in the responses of the two men. Surely the caddy would employ some finger-pointing. Or give a list of excuses. Surely Miles Byrne could find someone or something to blame for his mistake. Instead, Byrne said, "You want me to stand here and make excuses? There is no excuse. The buck stops at me. My fault, two-shot penalty, end of story."

And what about Woosnam? How loudly would the Welshman yell when he fired Byrne, the caddy who may have cost him his last chance at a major championship? Surely no one on earth would blame him.

The *Irish Examiner* printed his response: "With a superhuman show of forgiveness Woosnam did not murder Byrne."

"It's the biggest mistake he will make in his life," said Woosnam. "He won't do it again. He's a good caddie. He will have a severe talking to when I get in, but I'm not going to sack him."[1]

As the two walked together down the fairway to the eighteenth green, the crowd rose to its feet, giving them a standing ovation. Failure and remorse. Repentance and forgiveness. I think I've read that story somewhere before.

> *It takes great strength to ask for forgiveness,*
> *divine strength to forgive.*

Tip of the Day: When you start your downswing, shift your weight to your left foot while bringing your right elbow back down to your body. Practice it over and over and over. Except during meals and board meetings.

13

THE TRUTH ABOUT LYING

*If you pick up a golfer and hold it close to your ear, like
a conch shell, and listen, you will hear an alibi.*

FRED BECK

*If you think it's hard to meet new people, try
picking up the wrong golf ball.*

JACK LEMMON

On his way to the golf course a man saw a sign in front of a house: "Talking Dog for Sale." He smiled and almost drove past. But curiosity got the best of him, so he called the course, delayed his tee time, rang the doorbell, and asked, "Are you serious? You have a talking dog?" The owner looked him up and down, winced at his checkered pants, and said, "That's right, sir. The dog is in the back-yard. Go see for yourself."

The man lifted the latch on the fence, and, sure enough, there he was. An ink-black terrier just sitting there, its tongue hanging out to the side, its tail wagging just a little.

"You talk?" the man asked.

"Yep," the dog replied. "Sure do."

"So, what's your story?"

The dog looked up and said, "Well, I discovered my gift of talking when I was a young pup. I wanted to help the government, so I told the CIA about my gift. In no time, I found myself jetting around the world, sitting in opulent rooms with spies and world leaders. I guess no one figured a dog would be eavesdropping. It went so well that I was voted 'Most Valuable Spy' eight years running. But the lifestyle exhausted me. I hardly knew my friends. I wasn't getting any younger, and it was time to settle down. So I've been at the airport doing undercover work, mostly wandering near suspicious characters and listening in on surreptitious conversations. I uncovered some remarkable dealings there and was awarded a batch of medals. But finally I got married, had a litter of puppies, and called it quits. I'm retired now. I'm exceedingly happy."

The guy stood there amazed. "Uh, thanks," was all he could say.

He rang the doorbell again and asked the owner, "What do you want for the dog?"

"Ten bucks," said the owner.

"Ten bucks," said the man. "Are you out of your mind? This dog is amazing. This dog has traveled the world as a spy. He's brilliant. Why on earth are you selling him so cheap?"

"'Cause he's a liar," said the owner. "He didn't do any of that stuff!"

Improving Your Lie

Nobody likes a liar, but most admit to being one. Studies show that 97.8 percent of people have told a lie. I think the other 2.2 percent were lying.

Parents lie. We say, "Keep doing that and your face will stay that way." Or, "We sent old Rover to live at a big farm where he can run free."

Most golfers know an alleged sandbagger, one who intentionally inflates his score to raise his handicap to earn more strokes at tournaments. One video even teaches "Ten ways to tell if a fellow golfer is cheating." Lies are common at Christmas. Lies like, "Thanks! I love this sweater."

In one poll of college students, 79 percent said that when it came to telling the truth, they were most likely to trust their grandparents' generation, 68 percent said they trusted their parents' generation, only 25 percent trusted their generation.[1]

Yet in a study of 2,015 avid golfers who were given 15 common golf scenarios, the bulk said they never bend golf's most stringent rules.[2] When asked if they would count the stroke when swinging at a ball in the rough and missing it completely, 87 percent said they would. The golf course is one of the few remaining places that demands complete integrity, and, for the most part, gets it.

According to another study, those who live with integrity experience less stress, better health, and longer lives. When 110 people aged 18 to 71 agreed to take a lie detector test once a week for ten weeks, those who lied the least reported better mental and physical health, stronger relationships, less trouble sleeping, less tension, fewer headaches, and fewer sore throats.[3]

The apostle Peter was right. He wrote, "If you want to enjoy life and see many happy days, keep your tongue from speaking evil and your lips from telling lies. Turn away from evil and do good."[4]

The truth will set you free, the Bible says, speaking of our spiritual health. And we shouldn't be surprised when it also brings fewer sore throats, better sleep, and less explaining to do when a friend looks over our scorecard in the clubhouse.

Integrity should characterize our golf game and our life. I'm sure our talking dog would agree. And next time you receive an ugly Christmas sweater, just say, "Thanks for not buying me the matching pants."

How well you sleep may depend on how little you lie.

Tip of the Day: Count every stroke, always. Bob Hope joked, "Isn't it fun to go out on the course and lie in the sun?" But when we lie, we cheat not only our partners but ourselves. I'd rather get an honest 104 and try to beat it than write down 84 knowing I never will.

14

LOST AND FOUND

*I found out that all the important lessons of life are contained
in the three rules for achieving a perfect golf swing: 1. Keep
your head down. 2. Follow through. 3. Be born with money.*

P.J. O'ROURKE

*The object of golf is not just to win. It is to
play like a gentleman, and win.*

PHIL MICKELSON

One old duffer I know has given up on golf altogether. He doesn't mind hitting a ball now and then, but if you're standing near him when he swings, you'll notice he purposely aims for the creek. And when the ball goes where he intended, he feigns disappointment. "You go on ahead," he says. "I'll catch up later." But he won't catch up. He will slide his gold-colored ball retriever from his bag and slip over the edge of the bank where the shanked balls hide.

Everything in his bag has failed him except for his trusty golden retriever.

It is a sad thing to watch the golfer become a gatherer.

I asked him one day about the secret to finding lost golf balls. It was as though I'd asked a fisherman to show me his favorite fishing hole. He squinted at me suspiciously.

"I'm not gonna follow you in there," I assured him.

He whispered some things. Top secret things. "Here's the deal. You drag your feet. Like this," he said, showing me his signature shuffle. "And you wear bigger shoes than you need. They cover more ground. I'd say 25 percent of all the balls I find I've discovered with my feet. I used to bring a rake out here to pull them out of the creek, but the manager made me stop."

He seemed surprised I wasn't taking notes. You would have thought he'd uncovered Coca-Cola's secret recipe or the directions to Atlantis.

"When you golf, you gotta notice where people lose balls. You keep track. Then you go back later, after they're gone. I wear gloves and long pants. They plant thorns on purpose, you know? Stinging nettles. Poison oak. You can't be too careful. I don't bother with the creek much. It's too murky. I shuffle my feet along close to it, but I face away. I look up the bank, the opposite direction from where the balls come in."

"Do you ever fall in?"

It was like asking a fisherman if he'd ever hooked himself in the ear.

"Oya," he said, laughing. "Many times. See this?" He rolled up his pant legs. His shoes were wet and mucky; his calves were laced with thorny scratches.

"Is it worth it?" I asked.

At first he wouldn't even dignify my question with a response, but then he couldn't stop himself. His eyes were darting around now. "I haven't bought a sleeve in twenty years."

"What's the craziest thing you've done to find balls?"

"Sometimes I lie right down in the grass," he confessed, his eyes far away now, as if remembering his first kiss. "I roll around. I don't do it so much anymore though."

"Why's that?"

"Thorns. Rocks. Arthritis."

"How many balls do you think you've found?"

He chuckled humbly, but I knew it was the one question he was dying to answer.

"Three thousand last summer. They're in my garage. Buckets of them."

"Did you find any with my name on them? You know, Callaway?"

He stopped chuckling.

"Those are mine," I said. "You should give 'em back."

He laughed.

"What's the strangest, most bizarre golf ball you've ever found?"

He had to think about that one. "I found one with a fish on it," he said. "I think it was someone's way of sharing the gospel. There were words on the other side. It said, 'I once was lost but now I'm found.'"

The Big Picture

When I was a kid, a picture hung on our wall that sparked a longing deep within. If I shut my eyes tightly, I can see it even now. It was of the Good Shepherd hugging a lost sheep to his chest. Beneath it a verse of Scripture stood out, forever reminding me of the extraordinary lengths Jesus went to redeem lost sheep like me: "For the Son of man has come to seek and to save those who are lost" (Luke 19:10).

Though I cannot understand it, he somehow found me worth looking for. No distance was too far for him to travel. No price was too high for him to pay. The Creator of the universe came to earth as a creature. He came to die that we might live with him forever. He came because he would rather die than live without us.

What is left for us but to live thankful lives, passing God's grace along every day?

I think the dear old duffer on our golf course would agree. This morning when I arrived at work I found half a dozen golf balls on my desk. Each one had my name on it.

Ask not what this world has come to;
ask who has come to this world.

> **Tip of the Day:** Before lining up, lay a club on the ground or take your stance and hold your club shaft against your thighs. This should show you where you're aimed. Stop looking at the water hazard and focus on your goal. If you lay a club down, don't forget to pick it up.

15

ROCKY ROAD

*Reverse every natural instinct and do the opposite of
what you are inclined to do, and you will probably
come very close to having a perfect golf swing.*

BEN HOGAN

Nobody cheers for Goliath.

SEVEN-FOOT NBA HALL OF FAMER WILT CHAMBERLAIN
AFTER BEING SOUNDLY BOOED

I'm not a huge fan of boxing or any sport that requires two con-
testants to beat the stuffing out of each other. Oh, wait. I enjoy
hockey. It's all fun and games until someone loses a tooth. Then it's
called hockey.

After another knock-out victory, Muhammad Ali said, "There's
not a man alive who can whup me. I'm too fast. I'm too smart. I'm
too pretty. I should be a postage stamp. That's the only way I'll ever
get licked."

In his prime, Ali faced a relatively unknown boxer named Chuck
Wepner. No one thought Chuck would last two rounds. But he
knocked down the champ in the ninth round. Though Ali won the

fight, Wepner did the unthinkable, lasting 15 rounds against the greatest boxer in the world.

A young man watched that match and was inspired. He too was an underdog. A troubled kid with a partially paralyzed face, he was expelled from schools and spent time in foster homes. Moving to New York City to pursue an acting career, he scored only minor roles. Odd jobs kept him afloat. He slept at a bus station and stayed at a flophouse with "hot and cold running roaches." But when he watched the Ali/Wepner match, Sylvester Stallone had an idea. Three days later a finished script sat atop his desk: the story of a down-and-out boxer without a chance, Rocky Balboa.

Stallone sent his script to producers. Nobody wanted it. To complicate things, his wife was pregnant, and they had just $107 in the bank. Unable to feed his dog, Butkus, he sold him for $40.

Then came the call. "We'll give you $125,000 for the *Rocky* script." Stallone was ecstatic. But *Rocky* was *his* story. He couldn't sell it and walk away. "Let me play the lead role and you've got yourself a deal." They shook their heads. A big-name actor had dibs on that part, they said. They offered him $250,000. Then $360,000. A small fortune in the '70s. When Stallone held his ground, they finally agreed to his demands but gave him a small slice of their original offer. When the check cleared, Stallone tracked down the man who had purchased his dog and bought Butkus back for $15,000.

Keys to the Candy Store

Rocky went into production on a shoestring budget, using hand-held cameras and family and friends—even Butkus—in the cast. *Rocky* grossed $200 million, claimed three Academy Awards, including Best Picture, became one of the most-beloved underdog stories of our time, and launched the most successful sports movie franchise ever.

But Sly Stallone's personal life was rocky too. "I was raised in a Christian home," he said. "Then I was presented with temptation and lost my way and made a lot of bad choices...All of a sudden, you're given the keys to the candy store and temptation abounds. Then I began to believe my own publicity...I admit it, I just lost my way."

After 12 years of a downward spiral, he said, "I realized it had to stop. I had to get back to basics and take things out of my own hands and put them in God's hands."

Following the release of *Creed*, he said, "This is a story of faith, integrity and victory. Jesus is the inspiration for anyone to go the distance."

In golf, underdog stories abound.

Ben Curtis had precisely one top-25 finish when he teed off for the 2003 PGA Open Championship as a 300 to 1 long shot. Four rounds later he claimed his first major victory, shocking the golf world, and leaped from 395th in the world to 35th.

In 2011, Jason Dufner approached the fifteenth tee at the Atlanta Athletic Club with a five-stroke lead and his first major victory all but in the bag. Then the wheels fell off. First he hit the water. Then sailed into a greenside bunker. Then three-putted. Meanwhile, Keegan Bradley scrambled up the leaderboard to force a playoff, and three holes later Dufner endured one of the most painful collapses in golf history.

For a time it defined him. The voices whispered, reminding him of each disastrous shot. But at the 2013 PGA Championship, with no one expecting he had a chance, Dufner quieted those voices one shot at a time and finally banked his first major win.

Divine Underdogs

When I think of underdogs, I think of Bible heroes like Moses,

Esther, and Joseph. When the prophet Samuel told Jesse that Israel's next king was among his sons, Jesse didn't even think to bring David to the audition. Yet the forgotten son was the one with the eye of the tiger. David was God's choice to face Goliath and rule Israel. And don't forget Jesus, God's Son, who became a man and handed death the ultimate knock-out punch and reconciled us to God.

We've all been discouraged. But these underdogs who faced overwhelming odds with courage, persistence, and faith inspire us. Remember Muhammad Ali's words? We can be like a postage stamp too. And stick to something until we reach our destination.

It takes courage to let go of things not worth sticking to.

Tip of the Day: Nutrition experts advise golfers to avoid caffeine and alcohol (both are diuretics and cause fluid loss) and drink lots of water. If you're a serious golfer, avoid large amounts of food two hours before your tee time. Instead, pack five or six small meals to eat throughout the day. If you're bringing a teenager, pack five or six bag lunches.

16

GET BACK

I've had a good day when I don't fall out of the cart.
BUDDY HACKETT

My friend Ethan watches the Golf Channel religiously, shadowing the latest tip, stalking the perfect club. One that will offer hope for his hook—something he prefers to call a draw. Last winter he texted me a picture of his spanking-new fairway 7-wood and belly putter. "This changes everything," Ethan said. I responded quickly, "So does a universal remote." But he saw no humor there. He is an intense guy who has stated his number one goal in golf: beat me.

When May arrived we split a cart, and he proudly test-drove the clubs. "I'll break 90 this year," he said. "You watch." So I did. But as the round progressed, it became clear that the only way Ethan would break 90 was to quit after 11 holes. He faced the sixth hoping to hook it to the eighth. He gripped that belly putter looking like a caveman hunting dinner. With his 7-wood he employed stances he had seen on TV: the open stance, the closed stance, the bow-legged stance.

Now, one of my rules, after "Never comment on another

person's outfit," is "Never offer advice until you're asked." So I bit my tongue until the seventeenth frustrating hole in a row, when he finally sought my advice. "I'm no expert," I said, "but I think you should return to the basics." I reminded my friend of Vince Lombardi, the legendary football coach. When too many mistakes cost his Green Bay Packers a game, Lombardi held a football high above his head and said, "Gentlemen, this is a football."

I encouraged Ethan to practice the fundamentals. "Stick to the basics. Don't torture your mind with a thousand thoughts. Start by checking your grip and your aim. Then keep your head down. Relax. Have fun. You have great tools, but they'll misfire if you don't get back to the basics."

"Okay," he said, addressing the ball as though he were about to parachute behind enemy lines. Then he commenced to smack shot number 122 into the creek.

Your Money's Worth

Two high school students invited me to teach them the fundamentals of this glorious and frustrating game. I told them my teaching rules: 1) you can't pay me to teach you, and 2) never complain when you get your money's worth.

On the way to the course I informed them that golf is a complex game. You can do 97 things right, then turn your wrist and your ball is in someone's living room.

On the driving range we set down three buckets of balls, and I attempted to acquaint them with the proper grip and stance. They weren't interested. They wanted to hit balls like the guys on TV. The first novice gripped his 1-wood and lunged at it. The ball did not move. His friend attacked the ball with similar gusto, hitting it 100 yards. Straight up. After several more torturous swings, each with similar results, one asked, "Okay, what am I doing wrong?"

I laughed. "First of all," I said, "neither of you is smiling. You need to. If you can't laugh, you'll never enjoy golf. And remember, this is a simple game. All you have to do is get that little white thing into a quarter-inch hole in the ground 400 miles that way."

I taught them the basics of grip and stance and positioning and backswing and follow-through. Everything changed. They were smiling and hacking and sometimes things went right.

"That's it?" said one as if he'd mastered the game.

"For now it is. Remember, the key to playing this game well is to keep doing the right things over and over until they become part of your swing."

"Can we get some more balls?" they asked. "We're out."

Get a Grip

My favorite Bible verses for golfers are these: "Take a new grip with your tired hands and strengthen your weak knees. Mark out a straight path for your feet so that those who are weak and lame will not fall but become strong" (Hebrews 12:12-13).

There are fundamentals in golf; there are fundamentals in our spiritual lives. We keep our eyes focused on Jesus. Being like him is our goal. We keep our head down, praying like crazy for strength. We keep a grip on the truth of the Bible, which provides wisdom to walk a straight path. We do the right things over and over, developing worthwhile habits until they are second nature.

My two high school friends are in college now. They have yet to make it on the tour, but both enjoy regular rounds of golf.

As for my Golf Channel friend, Ethan, he just called to tell me about his brand-new 9-wood guaranteed to shave three strokes off his game. Now it will take him *12* holes to break 100.

There are no substitutes for fundamentals,
curiosity, and teachability.

Tip of the Day: Thousands of golfers have had their game hopelessly ruined by complicating or neglecting simple principles. So practice the basics: Proper swing stance. Backswing. Downswing. Head down. Follow through. Practice small swings first. Go from little to big. Relax. Grip the club tightly only when throwing it.

17

THE MOST IMPORTANT SHOT

You can make a lot of money in this game. Just ask my ex-wives.
Both of them are so rich that neither of their husbands work.

LEE TREVINO

Golf is a lot like my spiritual life. It's full of "just-abouts" and "what-ifs." It's crammed with "oopses" and "uh-ohs" and the occasional "Doh!" The game affords me an unvarnished glimpse of my soul, and I seldom like what I see.

Of course, there are times of complete victory in my game. Times when my clubs say, "Well done," and the cup seems more like a basketball hoop. But recently my golf game has been a lot like the Old Testament. An unending series of detours, betrayals, tragedies, and fulfilled prophecies, sometimes interrupted by a miracle. Landing my ball on the green lately has been as easy as landing a Boeing in my backyard. The hole seems barely large enough to support the flagstick. I hit certain clubs and then check to make sure the number on the head is right. Could someone have played a cruel joke? Sometimes I am certain there will be no golf in heaven because Revelation 21:4 says there will be no more crying there.

My son Stephen and I were on a practice range, and he misjudged the distance to the mat. He has what you'd call a pretzel swing—winding himself up and then letting go—and when he swung his 5-iron, the head hit the artificial grass of the mat so hard that he bent it into a 2-and-a-half iron. Amazingly, it has become the best club in his bag. He pulls it out when golfing with friends and proceeds to send the ball screaming 240 yards down the fairway. The friends want to know what club it was. "A 5-iron," says Stephen humbly, showing them the number. "I held up on it. I didn't want to kill the thing."

But that's not my story these days. Two hundred and forty yards is possible with a 1-wood. Down a steep hill. With a stiff breeze.

A reporter once asked a pro golfer about the secret to his success.

"Two words," said the golfer.

"And what are they, sir?"

"Good shots."

"And how do you make good shots?"

"One word."

"And what is that, sir?"

"Experience."

"And how do you get experience?"

"Two words."

"And what are they, sir?"

"Bad shots."

As surely as we learn to walk by stumbling, we learn to golf by duffing.

The Secret

Here is my secret to better golf. It's a big part of the reason I managed to shave eight strokes from my handicap in two years. Ready? I began to carry a second ball. I did not use the ball to cheat with, I swear. I did not cut a hole in my pocket and slip the ball down my pant leg in the rough. Honest. I used it to correct what I had just done. When I shanked or sliced or duffed and no one was in front of me or waiting behind, I would drop another ball and try to correct what I had just done.

If I could count my second shots, I could master this game.

Better golf is about learning from our mistakes and pressing on. Failing forward, as they say.

And what is the most important shot in golf? The drive? The putt? The chip? While each is significant, they aren't the most critical.

Last week on a short 340-yard par 4, I took out my 1-wood and spanked the ball 250 yards...straight up. Despite my coaxing, the ball did not get in the hole. It came down 40 yards in front of me. So I shared some thoughts with my golfing buddies about this new experiment I was trying with a sand driver. They just smiled. Then I took out a 3-wood and, miracle of miracles, found myself landing just shy of the green, chipping up and tapping in for par. See what I mean by my game and the Old Testament?

In this case, the most important shot was not my pitiful drive. It was the next shot.

I'm not saying the tee shot is unimportant or recommending that you duff your first shot on purpose. But once you've swung there's no improving on that particular shot. There's only learning from it.

Some of the dearest saints I know have left me shaking my head, they have had it so rough. If I were in their shoes, I would have packed it in long ago. One man I golfed with lost his house to a fire, his daughter to a car accident, and his wife to an affair. Most would be hounded by bitterness and regret. But he takes the next shot. His secret is one of tireless perseverance, graced by gratitude. "God has been so good to me," he keeps saying. "Jesus is with me. I've got my eye on the goal, and I'm not turning back."

In life and on the course, you'll find miracles if you go looking. Some small. Some great. For my friend, a multitude of scars are reminders to simply take that next step. Reminders that with God's help, he's stronger than whatever tried to hurt him.

Persist. The truly great blunder is to stop trying.

Tip of the Day: Uphill lies make you pull the ball. So shorten your uphill leg and straighten the other, keeping your hips level. On a downhill lie, do the opposite. Straighten your downhill leg and flex the uphill leg. Practice this shot. Better yet, practice staying away from hills.

18

NEARLY FAMOUS

I miss. I miss. I miss. I make.

SEVE BALLESTEROS, WHEN ASKED TO DESCRIBE HIS FOUR-PUTT
AT AUGUSTA'S NUMBER 16 IN 1990

There are few things more entertaining than sports interviews. Because we've all talked before thinking. And sometimes over-confidence and unpreparedness are beautiful things to witness, proof that some drink from the fountain of knowledge; others just gargle.

Golfer Greg Norman once said, "I owe a lot to my parents, especially my mother and father." Alex Rodriguez of the New York Yankees said, "Therapy can be a good thing. It can be therapeutic." Charles Shackleford was famous as an NBA star, but also for saying, "I can go right, I can go left, I'm amphibious." After a pitcher hit baseball player Tito Fuentes, Tito said, "They shouldn't throw at me. I'm the father of five or six kids." I understand. We had three kids in three years. Things were a little fuzzy at times.

Speaking of kids, NBA coach Jason Kidd once said, "We're going to turn this team around 360 degrees." Thankfully, Jason was never a pilot. Perhaps my favorite sports quote of them all came from NFL superstar Joe Theismann: "Nobody in football should be called a genius. A genius is a guy like Norman Einstein." Perhaps Norman was Albert's little brother.

My dream as a 14-year-old was to see my name in lights on the PGA tour. What I lacked in talent I would make up for in other areas. When microphones were thrust at me before that final round, I imagined myself saying, "You know, my back is against the wall, it's crunch time, it's do or die, there's no tomorrow.

"I'm gonna bring my A game, stick to the game plan, take it to the next level, take it one shot at a time, keep my head in the game, peak at the right time, stay within myself, make something happen, read those greens, and roll in those clutch putts.

"Nobody expected me to be here; nobody gave me half a chance. I have nothing to lose. Sure, the leaderboard is crowded. The field is good. But they put their pants on one leg at a time too.

"I feed on pressure. I stay hungry. It's anybody's match. 'Never up, never in,' I always say. I'll dig deep, focus, gel, click, execute, fire on all cylinders, never give up the hole.

"It'll go down to the wire. A real nail-biter. A real barn burner. I'll give 110 percent. I'll show some poise. 'Keep it long and straight,' I always say. 'Drive for show, putt for dough.' And when I win, I will have left nothing on the course, because, let me tell you, there is no glory in defeat, there is no quit in me, my sights are on the prize, 'cause if you aim at nothing, you'll hit it every time."

And later that day, when the match was over and the clubhouse lights had dimmed, the media would see me sitting there, alone, head down. And I would say, "Someone had to lose today. Give him credit. He scratched and clawed, got the breaks, wanted it more than I did." Then I would break down in tears and say, "I'm here to announce my retirement."

The media would gasp. "But you're only 14. You can't retire." And

I would say, "Why, yes, I can. It was never about the money. I can't wait to spend more time with my family. I want to thank my parents. Especially my father and mother."

More Than You Can Handle

Clichés. You gotta love 'em.

But sometimes Christians like me are guilty of using them when we shouldn't. I say we put them to bed, lay them to rest, put them out of our misery.

Cliché 1: "Bless your heart." What we really mean is, "I have to love that guy because God told me to, but he drives me crazy."

Cliché 2: "I'll pray for you." Say this only when you mean it. If someone asks you to pray, do it. Right then. Or write their name on your hand and pray when you see it. I've begun doing this lately, and it benefits both the writer and the writee.

Cliché 3: "God will never give you more than you can handle." People rarely say this when they get their tongue caught in a revolving door. It looks good on a bumper sticker, but it's not in the Bible. First Corinthians 10:13 promises that God won't allow us to be *tempted* beyond what we're able to bear, but, trust me, when you lose five immediate family members in one year as my wife did, life hands you more than you can handle alone. It forces you to turn to the only One big enough to help you carry it.

Cliché 4: "God is good all the time." It's true, of course. His goodness never ends or changes. But avoid saying it to someone facing hardship. An ear that listens, a heart that hurts, a mouth that is shut, and a shoulder that is soft are never cliché. They're priceless.

Most clichés include an element of truth. But mostly let's stop using them. Take it from a retired golf star. I may be no Norman Einstein, but I do know that clichés are a dead end. Avoid them like the plague.

The first step to wisdom is silence; the second is listening.

Tip of the Day: When you putt, take one or two prac- tice strokes to judge the distance. Then keep your head perfectly still and imitate that stroke. Inside six feet, keep your eyes on the ground where the ball was sitting even after stroking it. You may want to listen for the ball to hit the cup. If someone yells, "Fore!" tempo- rarily disregard this advice.

19

DOGS AND CATS AND GOLF

*My favorite shots are the practice swing and the
concealed putt. The rest can never be mastered.*

LORD ROBERTSON

Today my wife and I took the dog along to the course. It's not
something you would get away with in most places, but with
the dog days (I know, I know) of summer a distant memory and
winter approaching fast, I knew it was okay. Apart from two other
diehards five or six holes ahead, we had the course to ourselves.

"Sit!" I commanded her (my dog, of course) whenever I took a
swing. And she sat. Other than that, Mojo was free to roam, roust-
ing out gophers and cocking her head at a lone muskrat chewing
weeds along the steep creek bank.

Dogs would find golf an easy game, I think. I'm surprised they
haven't marked it as their territory. For one thing, they are men-
tally prepared. Mojo hasn't a care in the world. Bad shots, or the
anticipation of one, wouldn't bother her for a minute. I got mad
at her for chewing a newly found Pro V and moments later she'd

weaseled her way back onto my lap with a lick of my hand and a wag of her tail.

Take that attitude onto the golf course, and you would be unflappable. You'd smack an errant drive and dive into the bunker with gusto, happily blasting it onto the green. You'd shank one into the woods and bound in there like you couldn't wait, smiling all the while, wagging your tail, sniffing in anticipation. As you stand on the tee box, your tongue hanging a little to the left, you turn around three times and punch the ball out there straight and true.

Dogs would never lay up. They would go for it and make it every time. They wouldn't know they couldn't, so they would.

Dogs would kill us if they took up this sport.

Cats, on the other hand, would fare poorly. They are an indifferent lot, easily bored. Dogs say, "Come on, let's go, hurry up, drive faster." They thrive on repetition.

Not cats. Cats would shoot par once and never need to play the sport again. If they showed up at all, they would preen themselves in the pro shop, disapproving of other golfer's outfits. Cats would give new meaning to "scratch golfer." They'd be penalized for slow play and wouldn't care. They'd refuse to wear soft spikes. Cats would cheat. They would sit on the line of your putt and refuse to move. They'd sooner die than go near a water hazard. And you definitely wouldn't want one near a sand trap.

When our children were small, they taught Mojo to sit, lie down, shake with the wrong paw. And though she never learned to golf, she's taught me a few tricks that have come in handy on the golf course. Here they are:

Wag the right thing. Perhaps a dog is man's best friend because he wags his tail, not his tongue. Golfers can be notorious for gossip, but those who are a joy to golf with live by the rule: Others should be safe when they're not around. Proverbs 16:28 says, "A perverse person stirs up conflict, and a gossip separates close friends" (NIV). First Thessalonians 5:11 says, "So encourage each other and build each other up." Wag the right thing.

Stay away from the rocking chair. Sometimes at night, with Mojo at my feet, I sit in my rocking chair and read the newspaper and then find myself talking out loud. I say things like, "What's this world coming to? Politics are driving me crazy," and she's thinking, *I sure wish he'd put down the paper and find me a bone.*

A good dog knows that newspapers are useful for certain things but that worry is like a porch swing. It gives you something to do, but it doesn't take you anywhere. The great thinker Yogi Berra once said, "Ninety percent of the game is half mental." Focusing on our worries and fears can destroy a round of golf, so stay away from the rocking chair.

Keep your head up. I know "heads up" is bad golf advice, but it's great life advice. When my son came through the front door recently, I could tell how badly he'd done on the golf course. But Mojo didn't care. She met him at the door with her tongue ready. She ran in circles, leaping in the air and licking his face as if it were aging cheese. Mojo didn't ask how many bogeys he shot or putts he missed. She just loved him.

Five seconds of this and my son's smile lit up like it was Christmas. Even a furry little creature can reflect its Creator with undying love and devotion that gives us bright hope and a reason to carry on.

I need some of that love right now. You see, my wife is calling. It seems Mojo just devoured the toe of one of my new golf shoes. We dare not let this sport go to the dogs.

You're better to leave people wondering why
you didn't talk than why you did.

Tip of the Day: If you tend to slice the ball, tee up the ball on the right-hand side of the tee box and then aim toward the left side of the fairway. If you tend to hit the ball from right to left, do the opposite. For a banana slice you can count on every time, drop your back shoulder coming through.

20

MY TOP TWENTY

My favorite hobbies are fishing, hunting, and
swimming. But enough about my golf game.

BOB HOPE

We read the Bible and talked about why I've been struggling.
My husband said, "You've got the game, but you're too afraid
of messing it up." So I came out today and I just had fun.

MINNY YEO, LPGA STAR, AFTER MATCHING HER CAREER BEST, AT 68

I don't know about you, but I suffer from attention deficit—
uh...let me see...oh yes—disorder. So after writing the last chapter, I decided it was time to leave the office. Out on the course, I got
to talking with my son and a couple golfing buddies about songs
that were undoubtedly written on the trials and joys of golf. We had
no idea so many songs were penned about this great game. Though
the general population thought these hits were about other things,
we who golf know better. See if you can add to my list.

TOP TWENTY GOLF SONGS

1. Carry Underwood—"Before He Cheats"

2. Dire Straits—"Sultans of Swing"

3. Pat Benatar—"Hit Me with Your Best Shot"

4. Jerry Lee Lewis (and the Yips)—"A Whole Lotta Shakin' Going On"

5. Hank Williams—"Your Cheatin' Heart"

6. The Beach Boys—"Good Vibrations"

7. Simon and Garfunkel—"Bridge over Troubled Water"

8. Elvis Presley—"All Shook Up"

9. Bob Dylan—"Blowin' in the Wind"

10. The Carpenters—"There's a Kind of Hush"

11. Patsy Cline—"I Fall to Pieces"

12. Porter Wagoner—"Green, Green Grass of Home"

13. Ray Charles—"Born to Lose"

14. AC/DC—"Shot Down in Flames"

15. Willie Nelson—"Blue Eyes Crying in the Rain"

16. The Beatles—"The Fool on the Hill"

17. ABBA—"The Winner Takes It All"

18. Sandra Bullock—"Hope Floats" (Wait a minute. That's no song!)

19. Aerosmith—"Get a Grip"

20. Harry Connick Jr.—"One Last Pitch"

And my favorite song after 18 holes? "Go for a Soda" by Kim Mitchell.

No such list is complete, of course, without a few songs that are referred to as mondegreens, songs we thought said something else.

- Johnny Cash—"I Walk the Creek"
- The Beatles—"Can't Buy Me Par"
- The Temptations—"May I Have This Stance?"
- Rod Stewart—"Some Guys Sink All Their Putts"
- Bruce Springsteen—"Born for the PGA"

I hope you're able to laugh a little when you golf. Sometimes golf makes me laugh; sometimes it makes me cry. I prefer laughter, as there's less cleaning up to do afterward. Here are some questions that help me smile when I golf.

- Why is the easiest shot in golf the fourth putt?
- Why are really lousy players the most likely to share with me their ideas about my swing?
- Why can I hit the wide fairway 10 percent of the time and a one-inch poplar branch 90 percent of the time?
- Why do bunkers beckon and fairways repel?
- Why are so few of us born with the natural ability to hit the ball and so many with the ability to throw a club?
- Why, when there are two balls in a bunker, is mine the one in the footprint?
- Why do I always replace my divot after making a perfect approach shot?

Humorist Will Rogers said of Bob Hope that he celebrated his hundredth birthday thanks to golf and laughter. "I ain't so sure golf contributes to longevity," he explained, "but any golfer that can't laugh at his own game would be well advised to write an early epitaph."

A few thousand years before the advent of golf, God brought the Israelites out of captivity and back to Jerusalem. The psalmist told what happened: "Our mouths were filled with laughter, our tongues with songs of joy. Then it was said among the nations, 'The Lord has done great things for them.'"[1]

And he has. May our coworkers, our families, and our golf partners see that joy.

A round of golf during which I do not laugh is a round when someone must have stuffed a handkerchief down my throat and tied me up, because I usually find myself snickering at some point—no matter what my score is. Of course I get in the zone sometimes, intent on the flagstick. But I've discovered I rarely record a respectable score when I'm not smiling often, thanking God for the beauty all around me, and yes, even humming one of those golf songs.

After all, one of the fundamentals of golf is fun.

Joy grows best in the soil of thanksgiving.

> **Tip of the Day:** When on the driving range, spend an inordinate amount of time aiming at the 150-yard marker. Develop the confidence to hit the middle of the green, and you're rarely down in more than three from 150 yards. If you hit a ball less than three yards on the driving range, leave it there.

21

HEART OF THE MATTER

If you found this ball, you're not that good either.

WORDS ON A GOLF BALL FOUND BY THE AUTHOR

*You need a fantastic memory in this game to remember the
great shots and a very short memory to forget the bad ones.*

MAC O'GRADY

For my July birthday, Ramona threw a cheesecake party, invited some old friends over, and handed me a birthday card. "Birthdays are like golf," it said. "The higher the score, the more we're tempted to lie about it." I opened another. An old guy has just teed off. "Did you see where it went?" he asks his friend. "Ya," the friend replies, "but I can't remember."

As my years increase, I am consoled by a close circle of friends who love to laugh. C.S. Lewis once wrote, "Friendship is the greatest of all worldly goods. Certainly to me it is the chief happiness of life. If I had to give a piece of advice to a young man about a place to live, I think I should say, 'Sacrifice almost everything to live where you can be near your friends.'"[1]

So on a regular basis, I meet with five guys who hold me accountable. Ron Nickel is one of them. When Ron was a young pup, a physician probed and prodded and listened to his heart. "Your cholesterol count is higher than the price of gas," he said. Ron loves few things more than a triple-decker cheesecake smothered in chocolate sauce. Ask him if he would like a little ice cream and he'll say no. He'd like a *lot*. But the doctor ordered him to alter his eating habits and get more exercise or he would be staring down the barrel of a heart attack ten years down the road.

One Tuesday ten years later Ron and I had a small disagreement. I won't provide all the juicy details, but it involved a misunderstanding and petty stuff like money. Before you could say, "Doh!" the silence between us threatened to turn the issue into something larger. I was mad. I hung up on him. And determined not to talk to Ron again until the year 2399. *Who needs friends?* I thought. And I immediately knew the answer.

Our golf course has a few lone golfers. They play at their own pace and like it that way. One barely stays ahead of foursomes, throwing grass in the air on perfectly calm days. He licks a finger and holds it to the breeze—on the green—moving as slowly as a deer through an anaconda.

Solo golf has its pleasures. I am often at my best when no one is looking. I'm as predictable as a Holiday Inn, hitting my longest drives and sinking every four-foot putt. But I miss out on so much.

"Friendship is one of the sweetest joys of life," said Charles Spurgeon, the old preacher. "Many spirits might have failed beneath the bitterness of trial if they had not found a friend."[2]

Wake-Up Call

One day Ron called. "Let's go for coffee," he said.

"Will you pay?" I ventured.

"You bet," he replied, laughing.

And so we found ourselves sipping slowly, talking of family and the busyness of life. Then Ron got serious. "My father-in-law died a few weeks ago of a massive heart attack," he said. "He spent the last hour of his life on a hospital bed, talking on his phone, repairing relationships. It was a lesson to me."

"Me too," I said, squeezing a creamer and choking back tears. "I'm sorry, Ron. I was wrong."

He was quick to forgive.

Three days passed. I was holding the fridge door open, looking for—well, for donuts—when the phone call came. Ron had just had a heart attack.

Shocked, our family gathered in the living room to pray for God's intervention. Before we had a chance to ask, God answered.

When it comes to having a heart attack, location is everything. Just ask Ron. He was a sand wedge from a fully staffed ambulance. Just for good measure, a doctor happened to be walking by—a cardiologist.

Over time we golf buddies watched Ron's recovery with interest. Not because we were hoping he had willed us his clubs, but because we love this guy. Ron's wife and children smile at his change of diet, but they couldn't be happier to have him alive. Me too. Ron's near-death has brought some changes to my life. I'm more careful about what I eat. And what I say yes to. This morning I pasted this to my computer monitor: "Since everything here today might well be gone tomorrow, do you see how essential it is to live a holy life?"[3]

I suppose real life begins when we face our own mortality; when we savor good relationships; when we place our complete confidence, our health, and our future in the hands of God.

While I was writing this chapter, the phone rang twice. After the first call my wife informed me the doctor would like to see me for a little something they call a physical.

I said, "I'm sorry, honey. I'm busy that year."

She said, "I've given birth to three children. You'll do fine."

A minute later Ron called. Looks like it's my turn to pay for a bran muffin and some sugarless, creamless decaf coffee.

We'll head out to the golf course together, where I'll stand behind him and watch where he hits the ball. Then I'll try to remember where it went.

If you have more than enough friends
you are either rich or a good forgiver.

Tip of the Day: Some golf so slowly it looks as if they are sweeping for land mines. Pam Barnett said, "To help your concentration, don't take too much time." Endless preparation on the tee equals too many conflicting thoughts. After a brief warm-up swing, remember one or two things you must do to hit it straight and swing away. Don't think of excuses until after you hit the ball. Here's my personal favorite: "I haven't golfed since yesterday."

22

SECRET OF THE YELLOW SHIRT

Although golf was originally restricted to wealthy, overweight
Protestants, today it's open to anybody who owns hideous clothing.

DAVE BARRY

I grew up below the poverty line, so the clothing of my childhood was passed down by four older siblings and a dog named Inky, who especially liked the shirts I wore, judging by how many sleeves were missing. In time, however, I began to consider myself a fashion expert.

And then I had kids.

They were fine with my wardrobe at first, but when my daughter turned 11, she spoke the immortal words: "You're wearing THAT? In PUBLIC?" I have no idea what came over me, but in a moment of sheer recklessness, I handed her my wallet and said, "Find Mom. Go buy me some clothes." So they did. Gladly. They bought me clothes that matched. And fit. Thanks to these two, I no longer show up in public decked in a turtleneck, knee socks, and a kilt— though the one place that won't expel you for wearing such attire is a golf course.

Most golf pros dress like gentlemen, but some stand out like a parrot at a penguin festival. "Golf," says rocker and 7-handicapper Huey Lewis, "enables me to dress like an idiot." Ricky Fowler and John Daly love florescent costumes. Even the great Jack Nicklaus donned a bright yellow shirt or sweater for the final round of some tournaments.

I always wondered if there was a story behind that shirt. So I went looking.

It was 1986 and the 50th Masters was underway. Though the Golden Bear Jack Nicklaus was widely considered the greatest golfer of all time, the five-time Masters winner's career was in retreat. Mired in an 11-year drought, some were calling him the Olden Bear. Few gave him half a chance. And when he posted scores of 74 and 71, most doubted that the 46-year-old would even survive the cut. But there he was on Sunday, tied for ninth, four strokes behind the leader. He was wearing his yellow shirt, not for fashion or luck, but for friendship and honor.

Hello, Craig

Eighteen years earlier, William Smith, the minister at the Methodist church the Nicklauses attended, told Jack the minister's 11-year-old son, Craig, was battling bone cancer. "The Nicklauses would stop by our house and sit and drink a Coke and visit," Craig's mother recalled. "That's how Jack and Craig struck up a friendship. When we knew Craig would not live, Jack came to the house and said to Craig, 'What's your favorite color golf shirt?' Craig said, 'Yellow.' And Jack told him, 'Every Sunday, when I'm playing—and you can watch it on television—I will wear a yellow shirt, and that's my 'Hello, Craig.'"

Jack took the golfing world by storm in that yellow shirt while a dying boy smiled and cheered. Craig passed away at the age of 13, and in time, Jack began wearing other colors. But just before the 1986 Masters, his wife, Barbara, suggested he wear the yellow shirt once again in memory of Craig. Jack hadn't won a tournament in two years, a major in six, a Masters in eleven. With four holes left to play and Jack an insurmountable four strokes back, that wasn't about to change. Or was it?

At thirteen he fought back with a birdie. The gallery buzzed. Standing on the fifteenth fairway, Jack asked his caddie son, Jackie, if an eagle would do any good. Jackie smiled and said, "Let's see it." And see it they did, as Jack made two spectacular shots and sunk a long putt. When the leader dropped a stroke, Jack was one shot behind. The gallery swelled. Over the next two holes he hit two birdies, and approaching the eighteenth green, his name sat atop the leader board. Jack's final putt sunk and the golfing world rose to its feet. The unthinkable had happened. In just four holes, Jack had gained five strokes. The man in the yellow shirt had achieved his greatest Masters victory.

When he met the press, many of whom had written him off, he joked, "I'm not going to quit, guys. Maybe I should. Maybe that'd be the smart thing to do. But I'm not that smart."

Then the tears came as he told them about the shirt and why the victory meant so much to him. The greatest golfer in the world had worn yellow to honor a young cancer victim.

Favorite Souvenir

For all of us who go looking, opportunities abound to show compassion, to love and honor the broken, the sick, the hurting. Chances are we won't hear much applause for it. Not down here. But the applause of heaven will mean infinitely more. Jesus told his disciples in Matthew 25, "As you did it to one of the least of these my brothers, you did it to me."

I have a handful of souvenirs. My favorite comes from an organizer of the Masters who read my little book *With God on the Golf Course* and sent me a yellow Masters flag, signed by none other than the Golden Bear himself. I showed it to my friend Ethan, who loves it, covets it, and periodically offers me money for it. But it's not for sale. "I'll sell it to you when you beat me," I tell him. But that hasn't happened yet. Then again, you never know. We're playing golf later today, and he's showing some improvement. Maybe I can throw him off his game a bit. I just may wear my yellow shirt and a kilt.

One of the strongest virtues is kindness.

Tip of the Day: There is great debate as to where you should place the ball before you swing. Most teachers advise you to hit it off your left heel. I've managed reasonably consistent golf by ignoring their advice. For a driver and 3-wood, place the ball off your left heel. But move the rest of your shots slowly back until your wedge is dead center. When you pull the ball from the bunker with a rake, do so off your right foot.

23

TRUE CONFESSIONS

You're looking up. That's your problem.

GRAFFITI ON THE UNDERSIDE OF THE ROOF OF CART 47 AT SEA SCAPE GOLF COURSE,
KITTY HAWK, NORTH CAROLINA

*My liver would like to dedicate this book to me
for giving up drinking and taking up golf.*

THE DEDICATION IN *ALICE COOPER, GOLF MONSTER*

I know of few places where we encounter our true selves more often than the golf course. I *heard* I was a sinner in Sunday school. I *knew* I was a sinner on the golf course.

A friend of mine who has a bumper sticker that says, "Work is for those who don't know how to golf," stopped by my office in late July. His face was tanned, but there was a paleness about his cheekbones, and he was tugging on his tie as though it were a noose.

"What's wrong?" I asked. "Your kids? Your wife? Did you just back over a cat?"

"Worse," he responded, rubbing his bloodshot eyes. "I went to see a golf pro. He showed me my swing. I always thought it was pretty good, but the video looks as though I'm shoveling snow. The last few times I've played, I felt like cheating to keep up with my buddies. I see why so many drink after they play."

Like a man who beheld himself for the first time in a mirror, he was unprepared for what he saw.

He's not alone. Here are three deadly sins I must face each time I'm out there.

1. *The craving to cheat.* Apart from Dutch Blitz at Christmastime, nothing in all the world gives me the urge to cheat like golf. When I hook a ball into the woods and find it behind a tree, everything within me cries, "Kick it three feet, you idiot! Who's gonna know? No one's watching. They're looking for the results of their own incompetence." In such moments I think of Bobby Jones's immortal words at the 1925 US Open. When asked why he had called a penalty on himself, he said, "You might as well praise a man for not robbing a bank as to praise him for playing by the rules." The penalty ended up costing Jones the championship.

2. *The blunder into blame.* It's not whether you win or lose, but how you place the blame. While playing with three other golfers in a skins game (for a ball a hole), a wicked wind came out of nowhere on my downswing, hurling my shot left to right. When finally I found the ball buried deeply in a shoe mark in a cruel, damp, unraked bunker, a little voice tempted me with a thousand excuses. I managed to ignore the voice but ended up with a double bogey. The only immediate reward I could think of, as my vulture friends unzipped my pouch and clamored for my brand-new balls, was that my bag would be lighter.

3. *The appetite for anger.* Maybe you're one of those who greets each shot with inner applause and a gentle cry of thanksgiving. Not me. Sometimes golf ticks me off. I don't curse the course; instead, I grow deathly silent. Some simply quit. Others grow violent, taking it out on their equipment. Or they abuse tee boxes, putting

greens, and helpless shrubs. One player became so infuriated when he chunked a routine pitch into a trap that he bludgeoned his ankle with his wedge until he drew blood. He then threw his club into the trap, dove headlong in after it, and proceeded to lie on his back, scooping sand onto his body and yelling.

I kid you not.

I believe that is a two-stroke penalty.

"Of the Seven Deadly Sins," wrote Frederick Buechner, "anger is possibly the most fun. To lick your wounds, to smack your lips over grievances long past, to roll over your tongue the prospect of bitter confrontations still to come, to savor to the last toothsome morsel both the pain you are given and the pain you are giving back—in many ways it is a feast fit for a king. The chief drawback is that what you are wolfing down is yourself. The skeleton at the feast is you."

If you ever doubt you are a sinner, referee church hockey. In high school I did this and found myself breaking up a fistfight between two pastors. When I banished them to the penalty box, one said, "When I play hockey I leave Jesus behind." I said, "Really. I didn't notice."

All have sinned. We all need a Savior. Last week, after I lifted my head and then watched the ball bump along the fairway for 30 yards, my friend Greg, who already gives me nine strokes a round, said, "Take a mulligan." Sweeter words are seldom spoken.

God, too, offers sinners like me a divine do-over. The miracle of grace. By simply admitting our sins and trusting him, we are forgiven.

The truth of 1 Peter 2:24 transforms us:

> He personally carried our sins in his body on the cross so that we can be dead to sin and live for what is right. By his wounds you are healed.

You have been chosen by God himself. You are God's very

own—all this so that you may show to others how God called you out of the darkness into his wonderful light.[1]

With our annual Dutch Blitz tournament approaching, that is very good news indeed.

Beware the high cost of low living.

> **Tip of the Day:** The player and instructor Paul Runyan advised, "Don't let the bad shots get to you. Don't let yourself become angry. The true scramblers are thick-skinned. And they always beat the whiners." An old Italian proverb says, "Anger can be an expensive luxury." So take a lesson from a rocket ship. Count down before blasting off.

24

BEATING THE YIPS

*Am I afraid of high notes? Of course I am
afraid. What sane man is not?*

Luciano Pavarotti

We learn so many things from golf—how to suffer, for instance.

Bruce Lansky, author

A friend of mine is deadly with a putter. He's as confident as John Mayer with a six-string. I envy the smooth pendulum motion. The squinty eyes. From 14 feet he beats me every time. But put him 18 inches from the hole, and he's 50-50. Give him a short putt, and the squinty eyes cloud over.

He's not alone when it comes to the yips—that enemy of disgruntled duffers and harried hackers. But there's hope. Somewhere out there someone is chipping away at the mysterious root of the yips. We don't know who he is or how much he'll charge for the cure, but we dare not lose hope.

What exactly do the yips look like? They are accursed involuntary twitches of the hand or wrist doomed to defeat putts, crush spirits, and cause normally well-adjusted golfers to twist their putters into pretzels.

Hank Haney charges $15,000 a day to help golfers solve their slice, patch their putts, and disentangle their drives. But there was a time when a bad case of the yips rendered him clueless as to where his own tee shot was headed.

The yips have also sabotaged the illustrious careers of Sergio Garcia, David Duval, and Kevin Na, who took a seven-year break from winning on the PGA Tour before his 2018 victory at the Greenbrier. "For some reason, I felt like it was my day," Na told CBS Sports. "I thank God." Na admitted, "I went through the yips." Did he ever. He went from being unable to take the club back to winning by five strokes.

My favorite yip story dates way back to the 1998 Masters when Mark O'Meara went straight to the putting green on Thursday after shooting a disastrous 74. Hank Haney said it was the most discouraged he had seen O'Meara in 23 years of working together. Haney started his post-round pep talk telling him it was going to be okay. But O'Meara knew better. He said, "How can I be okay?" He couldn't sink a putt from two feet out.

What to Look For

Haney knew all about the yips. They had almost caused him to quit the game forever, but overcoming them had given him the knowledge of what to look for. He noticed that O'Meara was looking to the right of the hole, so Haney helped him adjust his eye alignment parallel to the target. "He could tell himself that was the problem," said Haney, "not the yips."[1]

Haney simply helped O'Meara get his eyes back on target.

On Friday O'Meara began sinking putts, long and short, and gaining confidence. Of all the 1998 Masters highlights, one is shown

on television more than any other. It's of Mark O'Meara calmly rolling in a 20-footer on the last hole. The birdie putt gave him a one-
shot victory over David Duval and Fred Couples and became the
defining moment in O'Meara's career, an incredible feat when you
realize how far winning was from his mind that Thursday afternoon.

In life, some are uniquely qualified to offer us advice when
we encounter the "yips." Others offer bumper sticker cures: "Just
hang in there." "Everything happens for a reason." "Time heals all
wounds." When one guy told me my wife's health problems would
vanish if we just had more faith, I thanked God I was not a violent
man because I felt like slugging him and saying, "If you just have
faith, this won't hurt." Sometimes life *does* hurt. And when someone
has been there, has walked where we are walking, has endured a hur-
ricane, battled bankruptcy, or suffered sickness, everything changes.

For five years she struggled with depression brought on by grand
mal seizures. Barely able to go an hour without one, she longed for
hope. She believed God loved her, but where was he? She cried out
to him, but the doors of heaven seemed locked, the windows bolted.
She believed he was there, but he seemed like a neighbor borrowing
stuff and not bringing it back. She read in 2 Chronicles 32:31 that
"God withdrew from Hezekiah in order to test him and to see what
was really in his heart," and said, "Maybe that's me."

Today those years are a distant memory. Medication has helped
treat the source of her trouble. But the trials she endured during that
season qualified her to help others. Her story has been heard and
read by millions through radio and the books I've written. Not a day
goes by when someone doesn't tell us how she has inspired them and
helped them face fear and find hope. She is, of course, my reluctant
golfing partner, Ramona, my wife of 37 years.

God is called "the Father of compassion and the God of all comfort, who comforts us in all our troubles, so that we can comfort

those in any trouble with the comfort we ourselves have received from God."[2]

We've received comfort. Let's pass it around. As we set our eyes on the target, others just may find it too.

A smooth sea never made a skillful sailor.

> **Tip of the Day:** Don't chop your chip. Follow all the way through. Grip close to the steel and make your backswing equal your follow-through. Use the club that will put the ball on the green the quickest and get it rolling to the hole. Near the green, 30- to 100-handicappers should putt whenever possible. If you're higher than that, just throw the ball.

25

A CHRISTIAN GAME

I wish I was better at golf.

Boxer Arturo Gatti to his wife as they waited
for medical treatment following a bloody ten-round battle

Golf is, quite simply, the greatest game on earth. This is not up for debate. But if you should doubt me, consider these irrefutable truths: Golf requires of its players honesty, self-control, meekness, faith, hope, perseverance, and long-suffering and is, therefore, a Christian game. The rules of golf reprimand swearing, cheating, chewing tobacco, coveting your friend's clubs, or throwing your friend's clubs. And golf is played in a garden, where God intended us to be from the beginning.

Here are six sports that some people believe to be in the same league as golf. As you will see, these people are dead wrong.

1. *Boxing.* Unlike golf, you cannot discuss important issues while you are boxing, nor can you pick up your teeth while wearing a boxing glove.

2. *Hockey.* When a player goes offside, he does not stop

play and confess what he has done. That's what golf requires. Absolute integrity. I have loved hockey since I was three, but it is not a sport—it is war. There are no winners in hockey, only survivors. I have broken bones playing this game, some of them mine. I have been knocked unconscious and still suffer memory loss. I also suffer memory loss.

3. *Soccer.* The net is huge and the field is too large. There are guys with poor eyesight on soccer pitches around the world, running in circles for hours, faithfully playing their positions and yelling for the ball, unaware it's midnight. The game is over. The fans have gone home. If you run around after dark on a golf course you will fall into the creek.

4. *Football.* How can football qualify as a sport when the ball won't even roll straight? I appreciate that the players huddle for prayer before each play, but this doesn't compensate for the fact that four minutes of action are crammed into a three-hour game.

5. *Baseball.* Nothing happens in baseball. There are center fielders who have fallen asleep during games, unnoticed. Every pitcher is a "scratch" pitcher. In baseball you can take a player out if he's having a bad game. Not in golf. In baseball you get unlimited foul balls. Not in golf. In baseball you can hit a home run over right, left, or center field. In golf every shot must be straight over second base.

6. *Tennis.* I enjoy the exercise tennis provides, but whoever came up with the scoring system had flunked math. "Love" is not nothing. It is the greatest thing on earth. First Corinthians 13:13 says, "Three things will last

forever—faith, hope, and love—and the greatest of these is love." Besides, grunting while hitting the ball is simply unacceptable in golf.

My son read my list above and grinned. "Dad," he said, "golf is more boring to watch than baseball." I told him I would pray for him. Apparently he agreed with whoever it was who said, "If you want to take long walks, take long walks. If you want to hit things with sticks, hit things with sticks. But there's no excuse for combining the two and putting the results on TV."

I reminded him of nine more reasons golf is the greatest game on earth. With these, I rest my case:

1. PGA events don't feature loud music between shots.

2. My son plays golf with people four times his age.

3. Most golfers do not need a referee.

4. Tickets to see some PGA events are $30. Tickets to the NHL average $100, the NFL $200.

5. PGA players sign balls they almost kill people with. Hockey players don't sign pucks that go into the crowd.

6. Unlike other professional sports leagues, the vast majority of its tournaments are run by volunteers and designed to donate 100 percent of net proceeds to local charities. Last year the PGA generated $177 million for charities, and the all-time total nears $3 billion. I kind of like that.

7. You can golf with your children. And beat them. What's not to like about that?

8. You can play golf with your grandchildren. And beat them too.

9. When all else fails, most friendly golf games show some grace. It's called the mulligan.

I submit to you, my friend, that golf is a Christian game.

Whatever your age, whatever your stage, take time to play.

> **Tip of the Day:** Work out whenever possible. Depending on your age, this may mean juggling barbells or squeezing the remote really hard. But be active. One great exercise for golfers is simple sit-ups. It strengthens your lower back, something every golfer needs. Younger guys can do sit-ups while juggling barbells.

26

BEST ROUND EVER

If your opponent is playing several shots in vain
attempts to extricate himself from a bunker, do not
stand near him and audibly count his strokes. It would
be justifiable homicide if he wound up his pitiable
exhibition by applying his niblick to your head.

HARRY VARDON

I've had some bad rounds of golf. Some good ones too. But without a doubt the best rounds are those spent with my sons or my daughter.

It wasn't always this way.

My firstborn, Stephen, and I began playing this game together when he could barely lift a club. Through the years I watched our scores plummet dramatically, while my playing partner put on 100 pounds. When his brother, Jeffrey, joined us, the boy changed. He often became so irrationally mad at his little brother that I considered buying him Nerf clubs. They fought over rules, over scores, over duffed shots, over whether or not one breathed loudly through his nose while the other was shooting.

One day on a pristine par 3, Jeffrey hit the creek. He took it hard enough as it was, but when his brother whispered, "Sploosh," it pushed the boy over the edge. There was yelling. And threatening. And more yelling.

I tried to remain calm, to remind myself we all need a training ground, a place to discover the fact that we are dyed-in-the-wool sinners. For me and my boys, that place is the golf course.

Following the Sploosh episode, I tapped on Stephen's door and handed him a short letter. With his permission, here it is.

> Dear Stephen,
>
> I hope you know you are one of the most important people in the world to me. I also hope you will give me a minute of your time. I was frustrated with you on the golf course today. You got mad, and complained, and made things miserable for your brother and me.
>
> I'm sorry if I spoke too harshly. I was frustrated too. I should have remained silent. It's something I'm learning. Would you please allow me to offer some advice? When golfing, try not to take it so seriously. There are only six kinds of golfers: pros, those who have fun, those who are constantly frustrated, and those who can't count. We can't let this game get to us.
>
> Here's my suggestion: Count five steamboats after each swing. After the final steamboat, do your best to grin and think of the next shot. I just read of a pro in Britain who took a 19 on one hole. Kid you not. Next time you shank one, think of him. Think of ice cream. If this doesn't work, throw yourself on the ground and pound the grass. No. Don't. I've watched you do this. It doesn't help your game.

More than any of these things, honor others and apologize when you're wrong. I will gladly relinquish my car keys to you when you do.

I hope we can golf together until long past the time I am old. I won't cry when you beat me. I promise. May your shots be straight, your drives long, and your putts short. May your ball lie in green pastures, not in still waters. And may you follow our precious Jesus through every bunker and trap that life throws your way.

Cheering you on,

Your ever-lovin' Dad

The years zinged by. One day Stephen's mother and I waved goodbye as he left for Uganda to work with AIDS orphans. I said, "Couldn't he just get a high-paying job? Who's gonna pay for my nursing home bills?"

That night we crawled into bed, the lawn trimmed, the house cleaned, the back porch swept, and we couldn't give thanks enough that Stephen wanted to serve God. It was our prayer since he was knee-high to a LEGO block that he would find God's will and do it. Still, I missed the boy.

Most nights when we had finished a round of golf, Stephen would brush his teeth outside our bedroom door. If the door was open, he came in. Boys are easy to talk to when there's toothpaste in their mouth. Suddenly I missed those talks. I missed him thumping down the stairs, pretending he'd wiped out, just to see the horrified looks on our faces. I even missed the music he cranked up about 11:00 p.m. I missed him rolling on the floor with the dog and sometimes me and standing at the fridge together at midnight talking about our round and wondering where Mom hid the chips.

"Lord," I prayed, "take care of this boy. I know he was on loan, but we got pretty attached to him. Wherever he is and wherever he goes, go with him."

God heard that prayer. Still does.

For years we prayed for a strong woman for our son. God has a sense of humor. When Stephen was 30, he met Dallas, a world-record-holding powerlifter. She carried him over the threshold not long ago. Today he works with me, writing a radio program that's heard around the world.

And sometimes we find ourselves playing golf together again. Between shots we laugh at lame jokes and talk of struggles and the things God is doing in the deepest parts of our souls. Last week we tallied up our scores, and he had beaten me by a stroke. I was okay with that. I'm one thankful guy. I'm thankful for our other kids too. They'll make good doctors and lawyers. They can pay for my nursing home bills.

It's not what we grab but what we give that makes life rich.

> **Tip of the Day:** Whenever possible, play golf with your kids. I haven't regretted the days off work or the money spent. One of life's most valuable lessons for a kid to learn is that bad things happen to good people. They learn this on the golf course. Whoever said life was fair never tried to take three toddlers through a revolving door. Nor have they played golf.

27

NEVER GIVE UP

They throw their clubs backwards, and that's wrong. You should always throw a club ahead of you so that you don't have to walk any extra distance to get it.

TOMMY BOLT, ON THE TEMPERS OF TODAY'S PLAYERS

Actually, the only time I ever took out a one-iron was to kill a tarantula. And it took a 7 to do that.

JIM MURRAY

It's been one of those days when hitting a golf ball with a golf club was like playing the mandolin with a tennis racket. My favorite club in the sand trap was a rake. For the first time in weeks I had the dreadful inclination to walk off the course. To call it quits. It's taken me 40 years to discover I can't stand this game.

How bad was my round? When I got home today, I sat down and penned a poem. I couldn't help myself.

SEVENTY–TWO

I've stood before on the eighteenth green,
my gaze downcast and low.

For I'd dreamed the dream of seventy-two,
then hit a nine or so.

I can kick the ball from tee to green
in four and sometimes three.
But to do it with these stupid clubs
is an impossibility.

I can crank a ball three hundred yards
when no one's there to see.
But I shank a ball three fairways right
when someone's watching me.

Yet here I stand on the eighteenth tee,
my score at sixty-eight,
and dream the dream of seventy-two.
Three partners stand and wait.

I'm living well and eating right,
I've repented when I've sinned.
I study those instructional books,
There blows a favorable wind.

And so I stare the flagstick down,
my muscles taut with fear.
I try to shut the doubters out;
they whisper in my ear.

Those cherished thoughts of seventy-two
have now all come and gone.
I've yet to reach that golden goal
my heart was set upon.

For on the drive I topped the ball
into some frightful ditch.

I tossed a club into the woods,
I stifled language rich.

And then I hit six out of bounds,
then bounced one off a tree.
I'm lying now beside the cup,
tapping in for ninety-three.

Sometimes golf is a little like a fifth-grade romance. Take it seriously and you'd better run. It smiles at first and leads you on. Then it writes you a nasty note and takes off with one of your friends.

I have a brother who had the sense to quit the game before he got any good at it. But I can't. I have expensive clubs. My wife bought them. What would my kids say if I quit? My friends?

Lee Trevino wrote, "I'm not saying my golf game went bad, but if I grew tomatoes, they'd come up sliced." One frustrated hacker, caddie Huxtable Pippey, advised, "Real golfers, no matter what the provocation, never strike a caddie with the driver. The sand wedge is far more effective."

Countless discouraged people could have quit.

Albert Einstein was four before he spoke a word.

Isaac Newton was considered "unpromising" in school.

When Thomas Edison was young, his teacher told him he was "too stupid to learn anything."

Michael Jordan was cut from his high school basketball team.

Robert Gamez went 15 years, 6 months between PGA victories.

John Hudson grew up with an alcoholic father. Golf was his great escape. By the age of 16, John was shooting par with borrowed clubs and was advised to turn it into a lucrative career. Working evenings and weekends, he finally earned enough to buy the best set Wilson made. Two days later they went missing. His father had sold them for booze money.

John never bought another set, never golfed another round.

All his life that set of clubs had been a metaphor for defeat. All his life he had believed his father's lies that he would never amount to anything.

Past tears, John told me his story after I spoke at a fundraiser. "I'll be taking it up again." He smiled. Past failure and regret, he had decided to press on.

The apostle Paul had his share of regrets too, yet he wrote, "Let us throw off everything that hinders and the sin that so easily entangles. And let us run with perseverance the race marked out for us, fixing our eyes on Jesus, the author and finisher of faith."[1]

Life for Winston Churchill didn't get off to a great start. Born in the ladies' room during a dance, he went on to fail sixth grade. In one of his most famous speeches, he said, "Never give in. Never give in. Never, never, never, never—in nothing, great or small, large or petty—never give in, except to convictions of honor and good sense."

He went on to smoke more than 300,000 cigars during his 90 years of life.

Tomorrow I'll take Winston's advice. I won't take up smoking. But I will get back out there. Just think. If I live to be 93, I can shoot my age.

Relax. Never let the ball tee you off.

Tip of the Day: Resist the urge to overthink. Relax. It's one of the best grip tips for every golfer. A relaxed grip promotes club head speed and a clean strike. Hold tightly enough to allow you to swing freely while still controlling the club. If the club goes farther than the ball, you're too relaxed.

28

PROMISING HAZARDS

Golf is a day spent in a round of strenuous idleness.

WILLIAM WORDSWORTH

*But you don't have to go up in the stands
and play your foul balls. I do.*

SAM SNEAD, TO TED WILLIAMS, ARGUING WHICH WAS MORE DIFFICULT
TO HIT—A MOVING BASEBALL OR A STATIONARY GOLF BALL

E very golfer knows someone who measures the success of his or her golf game not by how low the score plummets but by how many balls are found during a round. It's a new handicapping system. "I'm plus eight!" no longer means you are eight strokes over par; it means you found eight more balls than you lost. It matters not how scuffed or scraggly the balls are. Each one counts, and finding them has become more desirous to the golfer than working on his or her game.

My friend Scratch can't understand people like this. The moment you toss a ball retriever into your bag, it's only a matter of time before you're standing in the middle of the creek with hip waders, a lunch pail, and a baseball mitt.

I was critical of such folk until Ron, Vance, and I took our families for a weekend getaway to a resort that just happened to have one of the highest-ranked courses on the planet a pitching wedge from our chalet. When we arrived and drove slowly past the course, our wives rolled their eyes a little. No, they rolled them a lot.

"We won't golf," I insisted.

"We'll make brunch every morning," Vance promised.

"We'll chop wood," Ron volunteered.

"Liars," the ladies said in unison.

But we were serious. We were there to romance our wives. I know you're surprised. I was too.

The next morning, while the girls slept, we guys woke up early to light the fire and crack the eggs. First, however, we thought we'd better go for a short walk and a breath of fresh air. Because we needed walking sticks, I rummaged around the trunk of the car and—wouldn't you know it—found a few short irons and a ball retriever. Ron just happened to have some plastic grocery bags in his jacket. In the wilderness, one can't be overprepared.

We made our way along the cart path that led to a shallow kidney-shaped pool that wrapped itself halfway around the green. Along the path the pool was picked clean. But farther on we could not believe our good fortune. The floor of the pond was littered with hundreds of balls.

Like mad men, we scooped them. One shoveled, another bagged, the other hollered directions.

Our original plan was to walk 100 yards and hit them back into the pond, but we noticed something. People who golf at such resorts don't use scuffed-up balls. They use Titleist Pro Vs. So we kept fishing and bagging and hollering.

As we scrambled to bag some more, I noticed Vance was not helping. He was staring wide-eyed into the distance.

"Look," he said.

Ron and I stopped fishing and lifted our heads.

Real Treasure

Ragged edges of sunlight had peeped over the mountains behind us, lighting the snowcapped peaks and turning them a brilliant rosy red. The autumn leaves below remained subdued in the predawn shade, awaiting the light. As the pond settled into quietness, the entire scene was mirrored in the water and framed by silvery dew on the fairway on either side.

It was one of the most beautiful sights I have ever seen.

The heavens were telling the glory of God.

I'd like to tell you that we stood there a little longer or rushed back to the chalet for a camera or our wives. Truth is, we got back to work, scooping like madmen and then lugging our booty back to the chalet while our wives slept.

In the kitchen sink we cleaned and counted our treasures. Four hundred and eighty balls. I kid you not.

As we scrubbed, I looked out the window above the sink at the mountain scenery and then back at my hands in the murky water. And I told the others a story my mother liked to tell.

A man found a $5 bill in a gutter and spent the rest of his life looking for more. According to my mother, he never saw the trees. He never saw the flowers. He never saw the birds. In fact, he missed a hundred rainbows and a thousand sunsets. All he saw was gutters.

"Always look a little higher," said my mother.

Ron and Vance seemed to agree. "Tell you what," I said. "I'll keep these balls so you won't get too attached to them." They rolled their eyes and shook their heads at me. Above us, the floorboards told us the girls were stirring. "Quick. They're awake," I said. It was time to hide the motherlode in the trunk. And make some brunch.

God dwells in heaven and in the truly grateful heart.

Tip of the Day: Aim at the tip of the flagstick. Former touring pro and skills instructor Wally Armstrong believes many amateurs come up short of the pin during their approach shots because they try to land on the green and then roll their ball toward the hole. Afraid of overshooting the pin, their muscles tense and they come up short. When scooping a ball from the water, aim just beyond it as light refracts.

29

UNBREAKABLE

*I always thought of myself as some sort of athlete
until I started playing golf a couple of years ago.*

JAMES CAAN, ACTOR

*Golf is the closest game to the game we call life. You get
bad breaks from good shots; you get good breaks from bad
shots—but you have to play the ball where it lies.*

BOBBY JONES

At a charity tournament, my son Jeffery and I found ourselves
paired with a lawyer and a stock car racer who had been given a
cart slower than ours. My son was 15. He could not have been happier. As we sped past this poor race car driver, all he could do was
swing his club at us. We laughed a lot that day. I even tried out a
few new lawyer jokes. When I learned that the lawyer worked with
young offenders, I asked him for stories, and he complied. I'll never
forget his observation early in our round: "I have yet to defend a
young man in court who was an avid golfer."

"Say what?" I said.

"Kids who grow up playing golf learn to follow a rulebook," he explained. "They learn discipline, respect, and etiquette. They learn that you are responsible for your mistakes. You repair your divots. There are absolutes."

Golf can be a narrow-minded, uptight, graceless game. Just ask Aaron Baddeley. He showed up 40 seconds late for his tee time at a PGA Championship at Oak Hill Country Club in Rochester, New York. Penalized two strokes, he began a swift descent down the leader board.

Sometimes I'd like to delete a few rules from the rule book, and add a few of my own:

- Because I've not had time to warm up, on the first tee I shall shoot until I believe I have reached my full potential.

- A ball in the water is temporarily out of service. I have been punished enough by losing it, so I will close my eyes, throw a replacement at the green, and hit it again.

- Whether or not a ball is out of bounds depends on the level of danger associated with playing it. If I perceive there may be snakes, guard dogs, or burrs that could cling to my shorts, the ball shall be replayed.

On a warm September afternoon, a friend and I decided to set our own course. With not a soul in sight, we teed off on number three and aimed for number six. Then we drove from eight to two, then back to four. It was a dreadful experiment. I lost more balls in four holes than I did all summer.

What's true in golf is often true in life. Those who set their own course eventually awake to their own folly. We live in perilous times where we have thrown out wisdom developed over thousands of years. We've tossed out the rule book. "Do what's right for you" is our adage. But could it be that there is an ancient rule book that exists for our protection, to help us thrive and flourish?

What About Gord?

Fifteen years ago, I loved few things more than a round of golf with my friend Gord Allert, teller of the world's corniest jokes. I opened the door for him once. He said, "Yesterday a clown held the door for me. It was a nice jester."

But Gord's career was no joke. He had scrambled up the ladder of a multibillion-dollar corporation. Four hundred people answered to him. Life was good. He had it all. A godly wife. Four great kids. A church family. A classic Triumph convertible and all the stuff.

But, without my knowing, Gord was doing what seemed right for him. He grew adept at spending money he didn't have. Nothing illegal at first. But that soon changed. Trusted with huge signing authority, he established a false company, sent fake invoices, and turned on a faucet of stolen money—hundreds of thousands of dollars—all hidden from his wife.

Then came the knock. The corporation had grown suspicious. Two detectives left him alone in a small room with an 1,100-page binder—the corporation's audit. While Gord's family frantically called hospitals looking for him, he was interrogated for 13 hours, then charged with fraud. How would he break the news to his wife?

Just before midnight he was told bail had been paid. Someone *did* know where he was. In the car, his wife, Liz, was waiting. He blurted out everything. The lying. The stealing. She sat in stunned silence. Then Liz took his hand and, on the darkest day of his life, spoke life-giving words: "I'm not going anywhere. I love you."

Visiting a close friend in prison is something you never forget. *This could so easily be me,* I thought. Gord had trouble looking up at first. "Few things drain your joy quite like living a lie," he said. "Can

God redeem this?" I didn't know. But as Gord showed an interest in the other inmates, he began to find the answer. "They're my kids' ages," he said. "Most don't have a dad of their own." Each morning in the common area, Gord read his Bible. The kids started asking questions, affectionately calling him "Dad."

Following Gord's release, God provided a home and jobs for him and his wife. Gord soon paid back every penny he'd taken. And today he's back in jail, leading a program that teaches truths of the Bible to federal inmates who are hungry for them.

I realized one day while talking with him that my favorite stories always involve redemption. And they often involve prison.

"Fifteen years ago I never imagined this," he said, laughing. "Me, an executive, turned prisoner, turned prison program leader. I'm sure this is where God wanted me all along. I was too busy doing my own thing to listen."

Gord knows a few things for sure. He knows that those who hunger and thirst for righteousness are satisfied. That true freedom comes by walking in obedience. That whatever we are facing, God can redeem even this.

God never forgets the sinner; he forgets the sin.

Tip of the Day: After a bad shot, try freeze-framing your follow-through and holding it until the ball comes to a rest. Short game guru Dave Pelz believes this allows you to self-analyze what you've done, recognizing the crucial differences between good and bad swings. Don't pose too long, of course.

30

HEAVEN IN AUGUST

*Now, here's Jack Lemmon, about to play
an all-important eighth shot.*

JIM MCKAY, ANNOUNCER

*If you don't drive a golf ball at least 268 yards, you will need the
U.S. Navy on your left and the French Foreign Legion on the right.*

SPORTSWRITER EDWIN POPE, DESCRIBING NUMBER EIGHTEEN
AT THE DORAL-RYDER OPEN

Sunrise comes early in August. I made breakfast that day, and with my brother-in-law Lauren, choked down eggs that were more like hockey pucks. To our west, the prairies stretched to the purple horizon. To the south, a network of lush fairways spread their green fingers across the valley, beckoning hackers like us.

As we strolled along the lazy creek of hole one, we spoke of the first time we shared a cart among the tall pines of a pristine mountain course. I had just married his wife's sister, so I was new to the family and hoping to make some inroads. What better place to do so than a golf course?

On one of the first holes, Lauren had taken out his trusty 5-iron and hit one of the most memorable shots I have personally witnessed. The ball commenced to take a miraculous right-angle turn and entered the woods. I had no idea a ball could ricochet off that many trees and live to tell about it. Lauren began having a stroke himself, holding the club as if it were an axe, chopping a hole in the fairway, yelling, "What in the...dog biscuits! Doh! For the love of Fritz!"

"Who's Fritz?" I asked. And he began to laugh.

I knew immediately I had found a kindred spirit. A brother from another mother.

For the past 25 years we had been inseparable. Lauren was without doubt the favorite uncle. He took an active interest in our kids, got down on the floor with them, bought them tacky little golf gizmos.

But that day walking beside the creek neither of us seemed to care much about our game. Lauren's slice had returned with a vengeance. His putts bounced; his chips wobbled. Yet there was no smacking the fairway. No griping. No hollering. Other thoughts clouded his mind.

I tried to distract him with the joke about the man who is about to tee off when a voice comes over the loudspeaker: "Will the gentleman on hole number one not hit from the ladies' tee box." The man backs away and then approaches his ball again. As he does, the same announcement comes over the loudspeaker. Irritated now, he backs away and then approaches his ball one more time. The announcement comes a third time: "We really need the gentleman on hole number one to move off of the ladies' tee box!" The man yells, "I need the announcer to shut up and let me play my second shot!"

Lauren shook his head. "That's the third time I've heard that," he said. "Tell the one about the angel and the golfer."

"Oh yeah." I was on a roll. "I told that to a pastor because he asked if I thought there would be golf in heaven. This angel appears to a guy who is golfing at Pebble Beach. The angel says, 'I can answer any question you want. Go ahead and ask.' The guy says, 'Are there golf courses in heaven?' The angel smiles and answers, 'Do you want the good news or the bad news first?' The guy shrugs. 'The good news.' So the angel says, 'The courses in heaven are so beautiful I can scarcely describe them. There are no green fees and carts are free. Golf balls miraculously jump from the rough and float on water. The cups are nine inches in diameter.' The golfer smiles and asks, 'What's the bad news?' 'Well,' the angel says, 'I booked you for a tee time in four minutes.'"

As I told it I wondered if I should have. But Lauren managed a half-hearted laugh. "A pastor? What did he think?"

"Well, he said he didn't want to go to heaven. It sounded boring."

"Boring? Where did he wanna go?" said Lauren. "There aren't many other options." We were quiet for a minute. Finally, he said, "It will be amazing. You know, I didn't think about heaven that much until...all this."

Seven Years to Live

"All this" began six years earlier when Lauren listened to a doctor's words as if he were in a dream. "Colon cancer...in the bone...We've seen people live as long as seven years..."

Lauren had been taking good care of himself since then, but the cancer and chemo were taking their toll. He was using that trusty 5-iron as a cane now.

Suddenly a ball landed in front of the green. We looked back. Someone was yelling at us to hurry up. So we moved off to a bench and sat there talking.

"Must be nice," said Lauren.

"What's that?"

"If your biggest problem is slow golfers. That would be okay." He was smiling. "I'm just thankful," he said, resting his chin on the 5-iron. "We've had a lot of fun out here, haven't we?"

"We sure have."

It was our last round of golf together. Each time I'm out there now and I see that bench, I think of Lauren. He wasn't quick to talk theology, but boy, did he live it. His coworkers adored him. He loved Jesus. And his wife and family.

Heaven. It looks even sweeter now that Lauren is there.

I think there will be chocolate we haven't yet tasted and colors we haven't yet seen. But the infinite pleasures there will take a back seat when we see the One who loves us most and knows our every longing.

Is there golf in heaven? I cannot think of one reason there wouldn't be. We'll move at our own pace there. I think Lauren's favorite club will still be a 5-iron.

Earth is the land of the dying,
heaven the land of the living.

Tip of the Day: When you hit the ball you shouldn't hear other voices. Think not on what is going on around you, on who is watching, or the awfulness of your last shot, but on where you want the ball to end up. Take dead aim. Golf is an easy little game. It's like writing. You just concentrate until sweat blurs your vision.

31

TOO OLD TO GOLF?

I still swing the way I used to, but when I look up
the ball is going in a different direction.

LEE TREVINO, ON AGING

I am approaching 50. I won't tell you from which side. But increasingly I'm playing golf with people who refused to give up on golf when their body started hollering at them, "Stop, you idiot! Go home. Watch TV."

One member of our club told me the aging thing has him perplexed. "I swing exactly the (bad word) way I did 20 years ago," he moaned. "But the (really bad word) ball doesn't go as far. I'm swinging just the same, but I'm pulling out a (exceedingly bad word) 3-wood where I used to hit a 7-iron." Then he said other things I won't repeat and thankfully can't remember.

For the most part, however, older guys and gals are a joy to golf with.

One Saturday afternoon my son Jeffrey and I had the pleasure of playing golf with two gentlemen, John and Earl, both of whom qualified for the seniors' discount years ago. I noticed some things immediately. For one thing, they weren't as eager as I was to impress anyone. I'm not sure the exact age at which you stop thinking you'll make it on the PGA tour, but they had far surpassed it. The impressive thing, however, was they still wanted to learn. In fact, John was trying to improve his putting stance. Earl said he needed to "come through" on his drives a little more. I discovered later that Earl was a 2-handicapper in his prime, but those days were in the rearview mirror.

John's swing, forged by decades of ailments, had him hoisting clubs only up to his belt loops and swatting the ball as if he were chasing a cat with a broom. Not once did we look for Earl's golf balls. "I'm too old to chase golf balls or move pianos or count calories," he said.

John had fewer clubs than I carry. No 3-irons. No 5-irons, for that matter. Lots of hybrids. He said he never carried more than three balls. But I noticed he had two different brands of ball retriever. In time, we found out why, but these two eightyish gentlemen were a delight.

They told stories of what things were like just after Noah got off the ark. They were short on criticism and long on laughter. Stingy with complaints and generous with compliments. They took an active interest in my son and showed great delight when he drove a ball 300 yards. Maybe they'd learned that in the grand scheme of things golf matters a little, but there are more important scores to be tallied.

That afternoon I found I was slowing my swing down a little. I didn't try to kill the ball like I do when I'm golfing with my son's friends. I thought to myself, *I love a game that allows you to play until you drop.* Like John and Earl, I'd like to be active long after the "best before" date on my kidneys. I'd like to be making a difference in the lives of others long into old age. Encouraging them, like these two encouraged my son. Still learning, still growing.

The Champions Tour

I am inspired by older people with active funny bones, imaginations, and lifestyles. Folks who demonstrate the twilight years can be productive ones:

Sam Snead won a PGA event at 52.

Leo Tolstoy learned to ride a bicycle at 67. I don't know if he played golf.

At 72, Greg Norman's mother, Toini Norman, was the reigning women's champ at Pelican Waters Golf Club in Caloundra, Australia. She aced the par-3 fourteenth hole.

At 78, Earl Dietering of Memphis, Tennessee, hit a hole in one twice during one round.

At 82, Leo Tolstoy wrote *I Cannot Be Silent*.

At 84, Thomas Edison produced the telephone.

At 90, Eamonn de Valera served as president of Ireland.

At 94, Leopold Stokowski signed a six-year recording contract.

At 100, Grandma Moses was still painting pictures.

At 103, Arthur Thompson shot his age on the Uplands Golf Club in Victoria, British Columbia.

The older people I admire are thankful people. They slow down but still live life on purpose. They don't long for the good old days; they're too busy leaving a legacy. Thoughts of death don't thrill them, but their hope is in God, and they can't wait to be with Jesus. Certain Bible verses make them smile. Like 2 Corinthians 4:16: "Therefore we do not lose heart. Though outwardly we are wasting away, yet inwardly we are being renewed day by day" (NIV).

At well past 90, James "Clyde" Dameron was the reigning champ of the Senior Olympics in Southeastern Virginia. Born the year

William Taylor patented the dimple pattern for golf balls, James shot his age twice at 75. He's done it so many times since, he stopped counting at 400. His secret to longevity? "I eat whatever I want and stay out of doctors' offices."

"I have been very blessed," he says, "so, God willing, I'll still be playing when I'm 101."

I suppose those who shoot their age do so partly because they don't act it.

One great reason to do the right thing today is tomorrow.

> **Tip of the Day:** Don't give way to the sin of comparison. You may never have a drive like the lean and lanky instructor. Do your best and leave it at that. Even Brooks Koepka loses. Ask yourself what will matter a year from now. Five years from now. A hundred years from now. Practice lots. Smile even more. Work with what God gave you.

32

EASTER VISITS THE MASTERS

I never pray to God to make a putt. I pray to God
to help me react good if I miss a putt.

CHI CHI RODRIGUEZ

If you wish to hide your character, do not play golf.

PERCY BOOMER, PROFESSIONAL GOLFER

Few golfers have achieved more success in our generation than Phil Mickelson, who has spent more than 25 years in golf's top 50. Phil was bit by the golf bug early, tossing a zillion balls into difficult places in his backyard and trying to save par.

Most golf fans know him as "Lefty" because...well, he plays golf left-handed. Few know that "Lefty" serves tennis balls right-handed. He holds a fork with his right hand. He writes right. In fact, the only sports-related object "Lefty" grabs with his left hand first is a golf club. The reason is fascinating. When Phil was one and a half years old, he learned the game by standing across from his father and watching him swing. His dad played right-handed. Mickelson simply mirrored his father's swing.

In Ephesians 5:1, we are told to do exactly that. "Follow God's example...as dearly loved children" (NIV). Or, "Watch what God does, and then you do it, like children who learn proper behavior from their parents" (MSG).

And what does this behavior look like? I think it starts with a little acronym that characterizes four pretty good golfers.

Grateful. Zach Johnson is one of only six golfers ever to win the Masters at Augusta and the British Open at St. Andrew's and perhaps the only one to do so with "Scriptures going in my head." He told the press, "I thank the Lord. I thank my friends. I thank my family...I'm just a guy from Iowa who's been blessed with a talent, and this game provided great opportunity." When he won the Masters with a record-tying 289 strokes, it was Easter Sunday. "This being Easter, I cannot help but believe my Lord and Savior, Jesus Christ was walking with me," Johnson said. "I owe this to Him."

Openhanded. Bubba Watson is one of golf's most enjoyable athletes to follow. Behind the colorful character is someone who credits Christ for his success. "Golf is just an avenue for Jesus to use me to reach as many people as I can," he says. This includes donating generous chunks of his earnings to charity. With his trademark pink Ping driver, he raises money for cancer research. Openhandedness comes from a grateful heart.

Loved. Webb Simpson, winner of the 2018 Player's Championship, has "sinner loved by a Savior" on his Twitter bio. Simpson is quick to credit God for his talent and slow to let it all go to his head. "I don't think about my gifting as that unique...It just happens to be that my gift is golf...I wasn't born to be a golfer. I was born to be a child of God." A favorite Bible verse of his is, "Live a life filled with love, following the example of Christ. He loved us and offered himself as a sacrifice for us."[1]

Forgiven. When the Official World Golf Ranking was first introduced, Bernhard Langer was number one. When he won his first Masters, he began to wonder, "Is this all there is?" Later he said, "I had lots of money, fast cars, a couple of homes, and a young wife. Basically, all you could dream of in this world…[but] there was still a void. It was almost a feeling of emptiness." A week after the victory, the onetime altar boy from Anhausen, Germany, found himself in a Bible study. "Guys were saying that we are saved by grace, not by how good we are," he said. "So I got my own Bible out and there it was in black and white." What he discovered was not a religion but a relationship with the living God. He discovered the joy of the forgiven.

Eight years later, on the brink of his second Masters win, he knew exactly what to tell the media if he won. And win he did. Incredibly, the win came three months before Jordan Spieth was born. Fast-forward to 2016, where Langer, 58, was once again contending, two strokes behind Spieth. Though he didn't win, Langer is now tearing it up on the Champions Tour, where he is ranked fifth. After a recent victory he was asked his secret to success after 60. "It's the sea food diet." He laughed. "I see food, I eat it. I like salad and veggies and fish, but I enjoy dessert too. I work out every day when I'm at home and have a light workout during tournaments."

Langer still wears the same size he did when he was 30.

And what did he tell the media that Sunday after his second Masters victory? "It's wonderful to win the greatest tournament in the world, but it means more to win on Easter Sunday—to celebrate the resurrection of my Lord and Savior."

Grateful. Openhanded. Loved. Forgiven. I think that sums up four who have faith in something greater than their own abilities.

Success is not judged by what we start
but by what we finish.

Tip of the Day: Learn to watch and imitate good golf-ers. You'll come to watch another's swing and know immediately how good he or she is. An older, wiser golfer told me that my right hand is merely there to stabilize the club. "Stop applying so much pressure with your right hand," he said. He was right. Single out one area in which you could improve. Go slow. A few aspirin might cure a headache; an entire bot-tle will kill you.

33

SOLOMON AND THE GENIE

Few things are more delightful than
grandchildren fighting over your lap.

DOUG LARSON

Our first three grandchildren were girls. I put golf clubs in their hands and knew in that moment that they would love the sport. But for now, they prefer books, so I show them pictures of golf courses. They say, "Read the story of Aladdin." So I do. I love to insert things into stories that take the kids by surprise. When Aladdin first encountered the genie, I told Eowyn, who is four going on twelve, the very first genie joke she'd ever heard. I had Aladdin say, "My first wish? I want a fur coat." The genie asks, "What fur?" Aladdin says, "Fur to keep me warm, that's what fur!" My granddaughter wrinkled her nose, looked at me, and snickered. I think she came very close to getting the joke. She said, "Bumpa, you're funny. I'm gonna keep you." That may be the kindest thing I've heard in years.

Here are three of my favorite genie jokes.

A man rubbed a lamp, a genie popped out, and the man asked

him for a wish. "I want all the ladies to love me," he said. So, *poof!* He turned into a chocolate bar.

An older couple was celebrating their thirty-fifth wedding anniversary walking on a beach. Suddenly the husband tripped over a bottle and a genie popped out. "You can each have one wish," said the genie. The wife celebrated and danced in a circle. "I would like to travel around the world with my dear hubby," she said. *Boom!* Everywhere, first-class tickets. The husband said, "I would like to be married to someone half my age." *Poof!* He was 112.

One more. If it's familiar to you, indulge me.

A genie appeared to a Seattle man offering to grant just one wish. The man said, "I wish you'd build a bridge from here to Hawaii so I could drive there anytime, get out of this rain, and play golf." The genie frowned. "I don't know," he said. "It sounds like quite an undertaking. Just think of the logistics. The sheer volume of concrete and steel is prohibitive. Pick something else."

The man said, "Okay, I wish for a complete understanding of women."

The genie scratched his head. Finally he said, "So would you like that bridge to be two lanes or four?"

Well, if you had just one wish, what would it be?

Straighter shots? Better putts? More money?

Anything You Want

One night, after King Solomon, David's son, had been worshipping, God came to him in a dream and said, "What do you want? Ask, and I will give it to you!" Imagine. This was no fictional genie. This was a visit from all-powerful God.

Solomon replied, "I am like a little child who doesn't know his way around...Give me an understanding heart so that I can govern your people well and know the difference between right and wrong."[1] What a response. The book of 1 Kings 3 tells us what God said: "Because you have asked for wisdom in governing my people with justice and have not asked for a long life or wealth or the death of your enemies...I will give you a wise and understanding heart such as no one else has had or ever will have! And I will also give you what you did not ask for—riches and fame...[and] a long life."

Of course, the rest is history. I just read an article that estimates Solomon's net worth was two trillion US dollars. Better still, Solomon ruled with wisdom. Though he was far from perfect, his people "were in awe of the king," the Bible says, "for they saw the wisdom God had given him for rendering justice."

What do you wish for today? Will it last? Will it make this world a better place? Will it please God?

Years ago an acquaintance lost his son to muscular dystrophy. Before his son died, a friend wheeled him through a mall, stopped, and asked, "If you had just one wish, what would it be?" He answered, "Nothing. I have Jesus. I have a mom and dad who love me. And I have friends like you to push me over the speedbumps." Then smiling, he said, "Besides, I know where I'm going. And there ain't no wheelchairs there." That's perspective. That's wisdom. That's awesome.

The boys have surpassed the girls in our grandchildren department. Six to four. I would love to take them golfing one day. I won't be able to afford that many carts, so we'll have to walk. Maybe I'll tell them genie jokes. Or I'll tell them of the day when they were small and I discovered the true meaning of love. It's watching *Peppa Pig* while the Masters is on another channel.

Your story is your best legacy.

> **Tip of the Day:** It's within the rules to mark your golf balls in any way that will give you an advantage. Some are helped by IDing balls with a straight arrow to help align their swing path on the tee or on the green. I once golfed with a man who hit the ball farther because he had printed a likeness of his boss on the ball. I do not recommend this.

34

WHEN YOU THOUGHT NO ONE WAS WATCHING

My dad's love was conditional. It was based on my
golf performance. My advice is to let your kids know
they are loved regardless of how they play.

BEVERLY KLASS, WHO WAS THRUST INTO COMPETING PROFESSIONALLY
ON THE LPGA TOUR WHEN SHE WAS TEN

The only golf instructor I ever had was my father. He liked to say, "Swing hard, son, just in case you ever hit it." That's what I was doing when the call came: "Your father may not make it through the night. You'd better come."

And so we canceled a tee time, gathered the grandkids, and sped to the hospital where Dad had been battling Alzheimer's-related pneumonia. The next morning, as the sun rose on his face, my father, a World War II veteran, fought earth's final battle.

Dear Dad,

We laid you to rest on a Wednesday under the wide prairie sky. Saying goodbye isn't easy. But saying goodbye to one who taught you to golf? One who loved you enough to say so? The tears came so fast I had to remind myself to breathe.

The night before you left us, the grandkids crowded around your bed and sang the hymns you loved. "Amazing Grace." "How Great Thou Art." All the while you held my daughter's hand, giving her another memory she'll carry for life.

That's what you were about, Dad. Memories. When I was a kid, I loved to sneak up on you and watch what you were doing when you didn't know I was there.

When you thought no one was watching, I saw you hit a golf ball in our backyard. You sliced it off a tree and whacked your car. I held my breath, knowing that for the first time in my life I would hear my father swear. Instead, you danced around using strong language like, "Oh shoot!" Then you snickered.

If anyone had reason to cuss, it was you. But somehow you lived life with an optimistic twinkle.

Your mom died when you were two, leaving you roaming your hometown while your father toiled in a furniture factory. Raised by crazy uncles in a home where the unspeakable was commonplace, you graduated from the school of hard knocks before entering first grade. But you never shouldered a backpack of grudges. Instead, you warmed our cold winters telling stories of a childhood I found enviable, one jammed with fistfights and sports and loaded rifles.

When you thought no one was watching, I learned how to treat ladies. I learned to suck it up when a par 3 was 198 yards for us and 110 for them. I learned how to honor them, open doors for them, put them first in line at potlucks.

When you thought no one was watching, I learned what was worth chasing. You avoided the deceptive staircase promising "success," investing in memories instead. You never owned a new car but scrounged to buy tent trailers and golf clubs for family vacations. You blew money on ice cream so we'd stay at the table longer. Watching your life, I learned that simplicity is the opposite of simplemindedness, and that those who win the rat race are still rats.

Rooting through your dresser last night, I found glasses, heart pills, and a reading lamp. I suspect you won't be needing them in heaven. In a file marked "Will," you'd misplaced a note Mom gave you listing your attributes. She made you sound like Father Teresa. "On time for work. A gentleman. Filled with integrity. Wholesome in speech. Loves family. Loves God." I guess it was filed correctly. It's the best inheritance a child could hope for.

Hours before you passed away, I had you to myself. You were struggling to breathe and my singing didn't help, so I thanked you for being a good dad. Then I opened the same old King James Bible I watched you read when I was a boy. Verses in Revelation 21 were underlined. I read them to you nice and loud, of that place where our tears will be wiped dry and our question marks straightened into exclamation points. By the time I reached the promise that your name is written in the Lamb's Book of Life, you were sound asleep. Friday morning you simply stopped breathing. No more tears. No more Alzheimer's. Home free.

Some kind soul said, "I'm sorry you lost your dad," and I smiled. "Thank you," I said. "But I haven't lost him. I know exactly where he is."

When you thought no one was watching, I learned how to die. With relationships intact, with nothing left unsaid.

Thanks, Dad, for loving my mom for 62 years. Thanks for taking me golfing and teaching me to fish. Thanks for majoring on the majors. And for a thousand timeless memories. Thanks for modeling how to finish the race, how to keep the faith.

Thanks for giving me a glimpse of what God looks like.

Each time I drive to our golf course, I pass your grave. And give thanks for your life. Tonight I'll lay flowers there and determine to live so the preacher won't have to lie at my funeral. To keep that twinkle alive. As you cheer me on, all the way Home.

Live in a way that when people speak evil of you,
no one will believe them.

Tip of the Day: Make sure you have a balanced follow-through. Your weight should shift to your front foot and your elbows will end up in front of your body. The follow-through will reflect what went on before. The same is true in life. The legacy of those whose word is gold, who model integrity and how to finish the race, will last.

35

THE GREATEST GIMME EVER

One of the most fascinating things about golf is how it reflects the cycle of life. No matter what you shoot, the next day you have to go back to the first tee and begin all over again and make yourself into something.

PETER JACOBSEN

Grace grows best in winter.

SAMUEL RUTHERFORD, SCOTTISH PREACHER

One gloomy day in early October, when the leaves are beginning to kiss the branches goodbye to litter the fairways with their red and yellow foliage, my buddies and I extend to each other uncommon grace, uttering words not heard in the heat of July, words that permit the demolition of golf's most sacred statute: "Play it as it lies."

It seems sacrilegious to some, but not to us. With snow fast approaching, we don layers of cumbersome sweaters, tug on unsightly mittens, and waddle over to the first tee. Our normally fluid movements are constricted, so we adopt winter rules that look roughly like this:

- Balls may be raked from bunkers.

- And kicked from behind trees.

- They may be lifted, cleaned, dropped or otherwise adjusted—until the golfer is satisfied.

- There shall be no such thing as a lost ball. The ball is merely missing and will eventually be found and pocketed by someone else. You are therefore warranted a free drop or do-over.

- Tomorrow the loser brings hot chocolate.

In the wake of the first snowfall, we sometimes play snow golf, a pleasing winter diversion which pink, orange, and yellow balls make possible. When the snow begins to drift, the color doesn't much matter. Not to boast, but I do hold the uncontested course record for the longest drive—well over 700 yards—something I accomplished by bringing the creek into play. If you hope to hit the same ball again, it may be necessary to peel off your beanie and listen for the sound of it dropping on the fairway.

The sheer implausibility of hitting a good shot makes us cheer for one another, and during these six- or seven-hole outings, I can't help thinking of community and grace.

You see, I spent too many years trying to measure up. Trying to do enough to earn my way to God. There's a lot of doo-doo out there. But true Christianity celebrates not what we do but what's been done for us.

"Because of the sacrifice of the Messiah," Ephesians 1:7-8 says, "his blood poured out on the altar of the Cross, we're a free people— free of penalties and punishments chalked up by all our misdeeds. And not just barely free, either. Abundantly free!" (MSG).

Most often, the game of golf is a nagging reminder of my

shortcomings. I duff. I hook. I fail. I stumble. Yet God's grace changes everything. This unmerited favor, this love that stoops and rescues, is the greatest gift I've ever received.

The Bible paints stunningly authentic pictures of the people God uses. I smile to imagine what a boardroom discussion might sound like if certain Bible characters applied to serve in some of our churches.

"Let's talk about Adam."

"Well, he seems like a good man, but he listens to his wife when he shouldn't. And you don't want to know what he wears in the woods."

"How about Noah?"

"He's prone to taking on huge building projects without a permit."

"What about Joseph?"

"Brags too much. Has a prison record. He's been accused of adultery."

"And Moses?"

"Are you kidding? He stutters and stammers. He has a bad temper. He's been known to hit things with a stick."

"So he's a golfer then?"

"That's another of his shortcomings."

"David looks like he has promise."

"Yes, but his kids are out of control and his wives are a handful. He's a strong proponent of loud music and dancing in worship."

"What about Solomon?"

"Has a good head on his shoulders, but it took him 7 years to complete the temple and 13 years to build his palace. I think he was trying to please all those wives."

"And Samson?"

"Hair's too long."

"Jonah?"

"Good runner, but he's disobedient and makes up big fish tales."

"Matthew?"

"Works for the IRS."

"John the Baptist?"

"He sure doesn't dress like a Baptist. Strange diet. Makes religious people mad."

"Paul?"

"Powerful preacher. Good leader. But he's short on tact and has been known to preach all night. Puts people to sleep."

"What about these others on the list?"

"Lazarus is dead."

"Zacchaeus doesn't measure up."

"Timothy is too young."

"Methuselah is too old."

"What about Judas?"

"Well, let's talk about him. He comes with fine character references. Good connections. He's conservative, so he won't rock the boat. Handles money well. Maybe he's the one."

God in his mercy chose to use the likes of these to shape the course of human history. Kind of gives us hope, doesn't it? When a friend offered me a gimme putt from three feet, I declined. Then I two-putted. The greatest "gimme" ever is the gift of eternal life offered through Jesus Christ. Let's accept it, living grateful lives, passing along the divine mulligan of grace.

Karma means we get what we have coming;
grace means we don't.

Tip of the Day: In life, accept the gimme; in golf, don't. Learn to tap in those short putts. That discipline will help you in tournament play. A *gimme* can best be defined as an agreement between two golfers, neither of whom can putt very well. If a friend offers you a gimme in a close match, thank him, then step up and miss by six feet.

36

THE FOLLOW-THROUGH

Don't play too much golf. Two rounds a day are plenty.
HARRY VARDON

Golf is deceptively simple and endlessly complicated;
it satisfies the soul and frustrates the intellect. It is at
the same time rewarding and maddening—and it is
without a doubt the greatest game ever invented.
ARNOLD PALMER

On the last day of October, Lenny finally empties the ball washers, tucks in the greens, and locks up the clubhouse. Most members are resigned to winter's fast approach, but a few fanatics refuse to surrender. Ethan is out there whacking golf balls at temporary greens. Next year he will beat me, he swears. But for this year, I'm safe. As surely as every round of golf comes to an end, so does every golf season.

Out my window gray clouds circle, threatening to pelt us with weather so miserable even polar bears are searching for travel deals.

Saturday was chilly. So chilly I saw two teenage guys walk past with their pants hiked all the way up.

I dragged the clubs from the trunk and spent a few hours indoors cleaning them up, tightening cleats, and washing balls my daughter and I found. Friends to the south ask if winter depresses the life out of me, and I tell them, "No. I'd probably golf less if I lived where you are. I wouldn't appreciate what I have. I might take it for granted, you know." It's a bald-faced lie, of course, but I'll likely tell it again this year. Truth is, I've already been asked to speak and golf in Hawaii come January. Sometimes God speaks very clearly to me, and I must say yes.

I hope you and I can golf together one day. Until then, I have four wishes for you.

1. Don't Forget to Laugh

This summer we played three games within a game. The first is "One Throw." For an entire hole, each player must abandon his clubs and throw the ball instead. It's surprising how often we laugh and how rarely the thrower loses.

We also enjoyed a game of "Reverse Mulligan." At some point during the match, each of us is allowed to use one Reverse Mulligan. If an opponent hits a ball from a fairway trap and sticks it 2 feet from the pin, or rolls one in from 46 feet, you cheer and applaud and then ask him to perform the miracle again. If he can't, too bad for him.

My personal favorite is "Yell," though *enjoy* is not the operative word here. During the match each player is allowed one bloodcurdling holler. It's not necessarily the best cure for the yips, but a round where Yell is played is one that is not soon forgotten. The best yellers employ suspense, standing close by when other players are about to hit the ball. Last spring I could hold a forkful of peas at the dinner table without trembling. This is no longer the case. At first I blamed age. Now I blame Yell.

Life gets serious sometimes, so don't forget to laugh.

2. Hang on to Hope

Golf is a bully. It will humiliate you in front of the class, punch you out, and steal your lunch money. But hope keeps us crawling back to the course, shoving another tee into the ground, thinking that maybe, just maybe something miraculous is about to take place.

In life, hope could be defined as **H**aving **O**ne **P**urpose: Eternity. Real hope vanquishes despair and gives birth to faith. Hope is not some vain wish that all will be well; it's the knowledge that—more surely than spring will come and those clubs will once again grace my trunk—Christ is risen, promising abundant life and eternity with him.

3. Pursue True Success

One of the wisest questions we'll ever ask is, "What does the Lord require of me?" Micah 6:8 gives the answer: "The LORD has told you what is good, and this is what he requires of you: to do what is right, to love mercy, and to walk humbly with your God."

I remember the day I received an email from a man who had accepted Christ as Savior and Lord after reading one of my books on golf. The sky was brighter than I'd seen it before. The trees were greener. And I knew I had been offered a tiny glimpse of what we will celebrate throughout eternity.

Perhaps true success is the privilege of being some link in the chain of making others homesick for heaven.

I once asked popular singer Steven Curtis Chapman what he would like to be remembered for. He said, "I would like to come to the end of my life and have my wife say, 'I saw his failures. I saw him blow it, but his greatest desire was to live a life that honored Jesus Christ.'"

4. Finish Well

Many nights while writing these stories I hopped into my car and drove northward past the Trochu Golf and Country Club where I spent half my childhood to a hospital where my father sat in the fog of Alzheimer's. Out his window was the third hole, which he and I sometimes strolled together. As I watched both my parents say their slow goodbyes, I became acutely aware of the brevity of life and how the toughest chapter can be the last one.

I remember one night in particular, amid a one-sided conversation in which I was running out of things to say, Dad's eyes suddenly lit up and his mouth opened. "Home," he said, and his face broke into a smile.

Neither Dad nor Mom were great golfers, but they were good finishers. They kept their eyes on the flagstick, and despite what came their way, kindness and integrity characterized them to their last breath.

One of my favorite golfers, without a doubt, is the apostle Paul. He said, "I have fought the good fight, I have finished the race, I have kept the faith. Now there is in store for me the crown of righteousness, which the Lord, the righteous Judge, will award to me on that day—and not only to me, but also to all who have longed for his appearing."[1]

May God give you the strength to fight the good fight. To finish strong. To keep the faith.

God bless you, my friend.

*Look straight ahead, and fix your eyes on what lies
before you. Mark out a straight path for your feet;
stay on a safe path. Don't get sidetracked; keep your feet
from following evil (Proverbs 4:25-27).*

Tip of the Day: Be there. I'm not talking about tee times, though we both love those. I'm talking about the Ultimate Appointment. One day soon we will see our Master face-to-face. I can't wait to celebrate with you as we cast our crowns at his feet. Until then, let's live for his glory, in his presence, all the way Home.

NOTES

Chapter 1: The Itch

1. Genesis 8:22.

Chapter 2: What Drives You?

1. Megan Bailey, "5 Christian Golfers Playing at the Masters," beliefnet.com, https://www.beliefnet.com/entertainment/sports/5-christian-golfers-playing-at-the-masters.aspx#J6RX9d9ioqh7LGJw.

2. Ibid.

Chapter 5: Mickey's Last Homer

1. John 3:16 NKJV.

2. Special thanks to my friend James Parker, Bobby Richardson's golf and fishing buddy, who pointed me to this redemptive story. To watch Bobby's phenomenal speech at the funeral, see https://www.youtube.com/watch?v=IJtRfrXHJsY.

Chapter 7: Escape from the Hanoi Hilton

1. Acts 24:27.

2. References for the three Bible verses quoted in this paragraph are 1 Corinthians 9:24; Hebrews 12:12; and Hebrews 12:1-2 NIV.

Chapter 10: The Spark of Failure

1. Rheta Grimsley Johnson, *Good Grief: The Story of Charles M. Schulz* (Kansas City, MO: Andrews McMeel Publishing, 1995).

2. Harvey Penick, *Harvey Penick's Little Red Book*, 20th Anniversary ed. (Simon and Schuster 1992, 2012), 149.

Chapter 11: I'm Number Three

1. David Ireland and Louis B. Tharp Jr., *Letters to an Unborn Child* (New York, NY: Harper& Row, 1974). Out of print.

Chapter 12: *Fore* Is Short for Forgiveness

1. A few weeks later when Byrne turned up late for a tee time and was fired, Woosnam said, "It's a shame...because he could be a good caddie—if he improved his adding up and timekeeping."

Chapter 13: The Truth About Lying

1. Laura Schlessinger and Rabbi Stewart Vogel, *The Ten Commandments* (New York, NY: Cliff Street/Harper Perennial, 1999), 270.

2. Max Adler, "Where Do You Fall On Golf's Honesty Meter?" Golf Digest, February 14, 2012, https://www.golfdigest.com/story/golf-honesty-survey.

3. David Ropeik, "Want a Healthier, Longer Life? Stop Lying," Psychology Today, August 7, 2012, https://www.psychologytoday.com/ca/blog/how-risky-is-it-really/201208/want-healthier -longer-life-stop-lying.

4. 1 Peter 3:10-11.

Chapter 20: My Top Twenty

1. Psalm 126:1-2 NIV.

Chapter 21: Heart of the Matter

1. C.S. Lewis, *The Letters of C.S. Lewis to Arthur Greeves* (New York, NY: Collier Books, 1986), 477.

2. Charles Spurgeon, *The Complete Works of C.H. Spurgeon, Volume 3* (Harrington, DE: Delmarva Publications, 2013), No. 1962, "The Friend of God," sermon delivered on May 8, 1887.

3. 2 Peter 3:11 MSG.

Chapter 23: True Confessions

1. 1 Peter 2:9.

Chapter 24: Beating the Yips

1. Matt Rudy, "Deconstructing the post-round practice session," Golf Digest, April 11, 2014, https://www.golfdigest.com/story/-by-matthew-rudy-they.

2. 2 Corinthians 1:3-4 NIV.

Chapter 27: Never Give Up

1. Hebrews 12:1-2 NIV.

Chapter 32: Easter Visits the Masters

1. Ephesians 5:2.

Chapter 33: Solomon and the Genie

1. Read the story in 1 Kings 3.

Chapter 36: The Follow-Through

1. 2 Timothy 4:7-8 NIV.

ABOUT THE AUTHOR

Phil Callaway has a set of Callaway clubs but no endorsement deal. He plays golf with his grown sons but still pays for the rounds. Phil hosts the daily radio program *Laugh Again*, heard on 400 radio stations (check it out at laughagain.us). He speaks at golf tournaments and for corporations, conferences, and churches. Phil's other books include *Laugh Like a Kid Again, Tricks My Dog Taught Me (About Life, Love, and God), To Be Perfectly Honest, Family Squeeze,* and *Laughing Matters*. He'd love to hear from you. To contact him, check out his books, CDs, and DVDs, or find out more about Phil's ministry, visit www.philcallaway.com.

YOU CAN FIND HOPE IN LIFE'S UPSIDE-DOWN MOMENTS

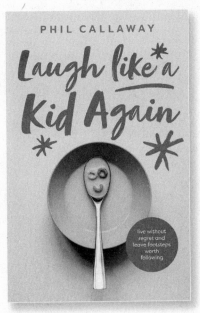

You've heard that laughter is the best medicine, but when reality hits, it can be difficult to muster joy.

Popular humorist and bestselling author Phil Callaway has walked through darkness, and knows well the downward spiral that can follow hardship and the long road back to happiness. In his newest collection of short stories, he brings a dose of laughter and levity to life's toughest moments. Drawn from his personal experiences, these inspiring and heartwarming accounts rooted in God's truth deliver real and lasting hope.

Whether you're facing a grave diagnosis, fractured relationships, financial burdens, or any number of bumps in life's journey, you don't have to let the grip of fear and bitterness take hold within. Learn to laugh again...with the help of humor-packed life lessons and encouraging insights.